Albert Shaw

The National Revenues

A collection of papers by American economists

Albert Shaw

The National Revenues
A collection of papers by American economists

ISBN/EAN: 9783337418885

Printed in Europe, USA, Canada, Australia, Japan

Cover: Foto ©Suzi / pixelio.de

More available books at **www.hansebooks.com**

The National Revenues:

A Collection of Papers

By American Economists.

Edited by ALBERT SHAW, Ph.D.

AUTHOR OF "CO-OPERATION IN A WESTERN CITY," "ICARIA; A CHAPTER IN THE HISTORY OF COMMUNISM," ETC.

With an Introduction, and an Appendix of Statistical Tables.

CHICAGO:
A. C. McCLURG & COMPANY.
1888.

COPYRIGHT
BY A. C. McCLURG & COMPANY,
A. D. 1888.

CONTENTS.

		PAGE.
I.	INTRODUCTORY. By the Editor,	7
II.	PROTECTIVE TARIFFS AS A QUESTION OF NATIONAL ECONOMY. By Professor William W. Folwell, of the University of Minnesota,	32
III.	SURPLUS FINANCIERING. By Professor Henry C. Adams, of the University of Michigan,	45
IV.	THE TARIFF AND TRUSTS—EXPENDITURES FOR INTERNAL IMPROVEMENTS. By Professor Richard T. Ely, of the Johns Hopkins University,	56
V.	SHALL THE INTERNAL REVENUE BE RETAINED? By Professor Richmond M. Smith, of Columbia College,	68
VI.	A DEFENSE OF THE PROTECTIVE POLICY. By Professor Robert Ellis Thompson, of the University of Pennsylvania,	78
VII.	THE READJUSTMENT OF THE REVENUES. By Professor Edwin R. A. Seligman, of Columbia College,	86
VIII.	THE THEORY AND PRACTICE OF PROTECTION. By Professor Jesse Macy, of Iowa College,	93
IX.	THE CERTAINTIES OF THE TARIFF QUESTION. By Professor, John B. Clark, of Smith College,	100
X.	TAXATION AND APPROPRIATION. By Professor Woodrow Wilson, of the Bryn Mawr College,	106
XI.	EQUALITY IN TAXATION—COMMERCIAL UNION WITH CANADA. By Professor Anson D. Morse, of Amherst College,	112

		PAGE
XII.	A GENERAL VIEW. By Chancellor Irving J. Manatt, of the University of Nebraska,	124
XIII.	STEAMSHIP SUBSIDIES AS A MEANS OF REDUCING THE SURPLUS. By Professor Arthur T. Hadley, of Yale College,	126
XIV.	THE IMMEDIATE TASK.—PROTECTION AND AMERICAN AGRICULTURE. By President Francis A. Walker, of the Massachusetts Institute of Technology,	135
XV.	THE TARIFF AND THE WESTERN FARMER. By Professor James H. Canfield, of the University of Kansas,	152
XVI.	INTERNAL TAXATION AND A REVENUE TARIFF. By Professor Arthur Yager, of the Georgetown (Kentucky) College,	161
XVII.	A PLAN OF TARIFF REDUCTION. By Professor Edward W. Bemis, of Vanderbilt University,	167
XVIII.	WAGES AND THE TARIFF. By Professor J. Laurence Laughlin, of Harvard University,	176
XIX.	THE SCIENTIFIC BASIS OF TARIFF LEGISLATION. By Hon. Carroll D. Wright, United States Commissioner of Labor,	189
XX.	CONCLUDING CHAPTER. By the Editor,	217

APPENDIX OF STATISTICAL TABLES.

		PAGE
I.	Analysis of United States Revenues for year ending June 30, 1887,	229
II.	Analysis of United States Expenditures for year ending June 30, 1887,	229
III.	Receipts of the United States by years, for thirty years, from Customs, Internal Revenue, and all other Sources,	230

Contents.

		PAGE
IV.	Expenditures of the United States for thirty years, analyzed by years,	231
V.	Analysis of Interest-bearing Public Debt, January 1, 1887, and January 1, 1888,	232
VI.	Disposition of Surplus for year ending June 30, 1887,	232
VII.	Accumulation of Surplus in Treasury, by months, from July 1, 1887, to May 1, 1888,	232
VIII.	Statement of Amount of Interest-bearing Debt each year for thirty years, with Amount of Annual Interest Charge,	233
IX.	List of Leading Articles of "Free-list" Imports, with Values of Goods Imported free of duty in fiscal year 1887. — Leading Dutiable Articles, with Values of Importations, Amounts of Duties collected, and Average (ad valorem) Rates of Duty,	234
X.	Table showing Relative Values of Principal Classes of Free and Dutiable Imports, etc,	239
XI.	Percentages of Total Duty paid by Leading Articles and Classes of Imports,	240
XII.	Analysis of Internal Revenue Receipts for 1886 and 1887,	241
XIII.	Table showing Estimate of the Effect of the "Mills Bill" on Revenues from Customs,	242
XIV.	Table showing Estimate of the Effect of the "Mills Bill" upon Receipts from Internal Revenue,	243
XV.	List of Revenue Reductions since the War, with Estimated Amounts of Reduction,	244
XVI.	General Features of our Export Trade for Fiscal Year 1887,	244
XVII.	Carrying Trade in American and Foreign Vessels for Fiscal Year 1887,	245

THE NATIONAL REVENUES.

INTRODUCTORY.

I.

The people of the United States are just now engaged, with greater interest, candor and intelligence than at any previous time in their history, in studying the problems of public economics. Circumstances all unite to make the times favorable for this study. There is nothing else in our national situation, external or internal, of such paramount or pressing importance as to divert the attention of the government and the people from the questions that are chiefly administrative and economic in their nature.

The European powers are of necessity so engrossed with affairs of diplomacy and international politics that they are obliged to adjust their economic arrangements to serve their political and military exigencies first, and only as a secondary consideration to enhance the well-being of their people. Our country, happily, is almost as free from the danger of invasion and foreign war as if it were alone on the planet. It has outgrown its earlier fears and dangers, and it need have no thought of war, except for those safeguards that common prudence might dictate even in that golden era of world-federation and universal peace that the poets foresee and the philanthropists strive to realize.

Nor are we embarrassed by the distractions of great domestic political problems of a fundamental nature, unsolved and irrepressible. The franchise rests upon the broad basis of manhood; we have no privileged classes; we are, therefore, exempt from those struggles between democracy and hereditary privilege that form the principal chapters in the recent constitutional history of the European States. Fortunately, we began at the point toward which the rest of the world is inevitably moving, and have been spared the agitation which always accompanies the process of broadening the political fabric at its base. Unfortunately, a "peculiar domestic institution," which was absolutely incompatible with our civilization and our political system was allowed to remain in existence, and a conflict of three-quarters of a century was required to eliminate it and to deal with the issues growing out of it. While it remained, the nature of the Federal Union and the supremacy of the Constitution were in constant and grave dispute. So long as there was lack of substantial agreement as to the indissolubility and sovereignty of the

Union, it was impossible to deal upon their merits with ordinary questions of national policy. The difficulty of adopting broad and permanent fiscal policies was made doubly great by the fact that the slaveholding States had not only distinct constitutional views to uphold, but had also an industrial system so radically antagonistic in principle to the system of the North that the prosperity of the whole country under one common policy as regarded trade and industry seemed impossible.

The South produced a few staple crops, largely for export, by slave labor, and had no desire for either diversified agriculture or manufactures. The men of the North, realizing the vast and varied natural resources of the country, its geographical isolation and completeness and its continental extent, had a vision of national economic independence through the utilization of natural advantages and the diversification of industries. They saw, at least more or less clearly, the close relationship between the growth of cities and industries and a complex economic life on the one hand, and the attainment of a high civilization on the other; and they were willing to make the sacrifices and pay the cost. Partly through the promptings of a fine spirit of patriotism, partly through the necessities and opportunities arising from wars in Europe and wars with Europe, partly through the superiority of

Yankee inventiveness and the unequalled productivity of American labor, partly through bounties given by the State governments, and partly through the operation of national tariffs so imposed as to discriminate in favor of American production, an agricultural North acquired factories, shops, and cities, imported industries instead of wares, increased rapidly in population, and at the same time developed a more intensive, more diverse and more prosperous agriculture.

It is quite impossible to determine satisfactorily what part one factor or another played in bringing about this result. They were all coöperating elements in this process of the rapid economic upbuilding of a people. To regard the discriminating tariff as a sort of *deus ex machina*, of its own inherent potential energy bringing about the wonderful progress from a simple farming people, few in number and of small wealth, to a great and populous nation with huge industries and splendid cities, is absurd. But that a young people with high spirit and a powerful awakening of national consciousness should employ the protective tariff system as one of various instruments and expedients for accelerating their material progress and attaining a completeness and independence of the national economic life that should in some measure correspond with and minister to the political independence of the country, is not at all absurd.

It was, under the circumstances then existing, the most natural thing in the world.

Whether such an instrument can be made really effective, whether it can be made to pay in social and political results—not to speak of economic results—anything which compensates for its initial pecuniary cost to the people who employ it, must depend wholly upon the people themselves, their territorial situation and natural advantages, the vigor with which they use other means for the national advancement, and, in short, the degree of potency possessed by those nascent forces in the young life of the nation that are transforming it from one stage of economic development to another.

There is certainly much reason to believe that if slavery had not existed in the South, making industrial progress beyond the simplest forms of agriculture impossible for that portion of the country, and making the free exchange of cotton and tobacco for the cheap manufactures of Europe the obvious and permanent policy of the planters, the country would have made a much more united, systematic and scientific trial of the protective system. For both cotton and iron manufactures the South had better advantages than the North. New England's seafaring industries and foreign commerce on the one hand, and the South's superior resources on the other, might possibly have reversed the traditional policies of the two sections and made the South more ardent for protection to home industries, and the North more inclined to favor unhampered freedom for foreign trade.

But sectional lines would hardly have been drawn. We should not have had two mutually destructive economic systems within our national limits, but rather a thoroughly homogeneous economic life throughout the entire country. Whatever use, under the circumstances, the American people might have made of protective tariffs, they would assuredly have made material progress " by leaps and by bounds." Slavery retarded American development. If it had been stamped out a hundred years ago we should have had a hundred millions of people and a national wealth almost doubled. It was the irrepressible national development that finally, bursting its vexatious bounds, overthrew slavery, settled the old dispute as to the constitutional right of the nation to build itself up as a nation, and made possible for the first time an economic policy freed from the reproach, just or unjust, of sectionalism.

If the North had not persistently fostered manufactures, in spite of Southern opposition and consequent fluctuations of national policy, slavery could not have been overthrown. The truth of this proposition is so obvious to all discerning minds that it needs no demonstration. It was the true instinct of self-preservation that guided, in the main, our economic progress, and made us at length a nation in reality.

The painful period of Reconstruction could not be omitted or bridged over; it was inevitable. But fundamental issues were settled. The constitutional dispute was at an end. The condition of a true "federative balance" had been attained between states and nation, and the people of all parties and all sections are to-day in substantial accord upon all fundamental questions affecting our political structure. Such temporary problems, growing out of the war, as those of the suspension and resumption of specie payments have been solved. The vigorous industrial life of the North is rapidly assimilating that of the South. We have thus, for the first time in our history, reached a point where, without serious distractions from without or any deep-lying sources of division within, we may devote ourselves as a united people, with harmony of interests and with recognized oneness of destiny, to the consideration of questions of national administration and economics.

The dawning of this fortunate period brings with it the demand for a new kind of statesmanship and a new kind of knowledge diffused among the people. The questions now uppermost require for their wise solution a large knowledge of public economy as a science. No nation has ever offered so vast and inviting a field as ours now presents, both for the study of economic subjects and for the application, through broad and well-informed statesmanship, of the results of economic study to the solution of practical questions.

It would be an easy thing to enumerate scores of vital subjects affecting our American life, as that of a social, industrial and political entity, upon which political and economic science can throw valuable light. A practical exigency has made the National Revenue System uppermost of all these questions.

By common consent and long usage,—the reasons of which our financial history supplies abundantly,—customs duties and excise taxes have been appropriated by the federal government as its exclusive sources of income, while direct taxation has been left to the States and their subordinate municipalities as their principal means of support. So colossal was the national expenditure during the period of civil war and immediately following it, that the government was obliged to consult ways and means for the largest possible income with comparatively little regard to the niceties of finance as a science. The national conditions made dependence upon home production more imperative than ever before.

The South had withdrawn from Congress, and in the construction of the new tariff there was something like unanimous consent to the most pronounced protective measures the country had ever adopted. But the decay of foreign trade incident to the war reduced the customs revenue to a minimum, and made recourse to a most elaborate and unsparing system of excise and "internal revenue" taxation an unavoidable necessity. For four years the aggregate income from internal taxes was twice as great as that from customs. But after the war there came a revival of foreign commerce with an accompanying increase in the revenue from customs, and there followed a gradual cutting off of the more burdensome internal taxes, until little was left of the once elaborate schedule except the taxes upon liquor and tobacco.

These sources of income have supplied the treasury so abundantly as to permit not only the most liberal current expenditure but also the unprecedentedly rapid reduction of the interest-bearing public debt, sixty per cent. of which has been paid off, while the annual interest charge has been reduced to one-fourth of the amount paid in 1865 when the debt was at its highest point. A cessation of debt payment resulting from the fact that of the bonds now outstanding none will be due until 1891, has been followed by the rapid accumulation of a large surplus of revenue in the treasury.

This situation,—in many indirect ways a very serious one,—has brought about a discussion that is destined to result in something more than the averting of an immediate crisis. The country has a mind to deal critically and thoroughly with the whole question of its national revenue system. If the protective idea is henceforth to govern in the imposition of customs taxes, the people desire to know more precisely what its objects are and how its arrangements actually affect the industrial life of the nation. They desire to learn what it costs, and to what extent and by what means its cost is distributed; and also what in kind and amount its benefits are, and how generally those benefits are diffused. They also desire to know the relative merits of the excise system and the customs system. In short, they desire not only to know at what points it is wisest to cut away sources of revenue in view of the present superabundance, but also upon what general lines an intelligent readjustment of the revenue system as a whole shall proceed.

Evidently these are not questions of a day or a single session of Congress. They can only be settled after much thought and discussion; and it is well that people should have the educational benefit of a thorough, protracted and popular agitation of all the phases of the complicated subject. These are matters for careful study and candid judgment, rather than for party clamor. They are matters about which the scientific students of public economy may have opinions worthy to be taken into account.

II.

The present little volume makes no pretense to be a treatise. It is, on the contrary, somewhat impromptu and quite unambitious. Nevertheless, it is believed that it will serve a useful purpose. Our political economists are no longer to be likened to "astronomers who have never seen the stars." Their attention is given very much less to philosophical abstractions and dialectical diversions than to the study of actual problems of social organization, economic welfare, and public administration. While the statesman's task is a different one, he is no closer to the facts of history and of the current life of society than is the economist of to-day; and he is learning to rely upon the student of economic science with growing confidence.

The last decade,—and more especially the last half decade,—has witnessed a remarkable impulse in this country to economic study and writing. The universities have become the recognized centers of this activity. Original investigation in economic fields has increased ten-fold. The study of political science has become prominent and popular at all our leading seats of learning, and the new work of the specialists in economic and historical research has begun to exert a marked influence upon public affairs. Not many years ago it was a common thing to hear men refer to the college professors as unpractical in their views, and to their political economy as a "science based on assumptions."

But there has come a change. The method and spirit of economic study has been greatly transformed. It can no longer be said, if ever it was said truly, that all our college graduates are free-traders when they leave school by virtue of a few easy and captivating syllogisms learned from their professors, and that all become protectionists a few years later by virtue of their contact with affairs and their participation in the actual economic life of the nation. Some college teaching of economics may still be as shallow and as unrelated to the facts of history and the life of nations as some college teaching formerly was; but the best teaching is open to no such reproach, and fortunately there is now much of the thorough and truly scientific instruction.

It has occurred to the writer that the opinions of a number of our American economists, chiefly university professors, upon phases general and particular of the national revenue situation, might just at this time be read with interest and profit. This collection of brief essays is the result of that thought. The papers are not elaborate studies. They were sent in response to requests which did not call for very extended or laborious replies. It was believed that the expressions taken as a whole would reveal the trend of thought among our foremost economic students, and would also help the average citizen to find the main bearings of subjects the intelligent approach to which puzzles very many. Whether the result justifies that anticipation, the reader must decide for himself. The collection of the papers has involved no little correspondence, and the attempt was made to secure some range and variety by suggesting special phases for treatment by particular individuals. The following general letter explanatory of the plan was also sent out:

"The people of the United States seem to be more generally and thoroughly interested just now than for many years past in the problems of national taxation. Candid discussion of these problems upon their merits, without reference to supposed party advantage, and without the bias of class interest or locality interest, is unfortunately too rare. I am persuaded that the views of our prominent political economists would at this time receive marked attention and exert a valuable influence. The importance of the numerous writings in general or special fields of finance and administration that have recently emanated from the American universities, is recognized at home and abroad, and the country is turning to the schools of political science, as never before, for light and aid in questions of practical statesmanship.

"After the holiday recess Congress must grapple in earnest the economic problems of the day. They are not to be finally adjusted by any mere makeshift, nor are they to be very quickly settled in one way or in another. An unusual number of men in public life as well as of private citizens are in an inquiring frame of mind and are open to conviction. It is my purpose to secure expressions of opinion from a score or more of those economists who are well known as writers and instructors, who are versed in the principles of taxation, and who know the economic experience of other countries as well as the history and present condition of our own national finances.

"It is perhaps to be preferred that these brief papers should give more prominence to conclusions than to the methods pursued in reaching them. I prefer not to present a list of questions for categorical reply, although I shall be glad, of course, to have the statements as frank and specific in their prescriptions as the writers may be ready and willing to make them It is not my plan to pit different economic schools against one another, or to obtain material for controversial uses. I confidently hope to secure a series of brief statements or papers that will as a whole greatly aid the intelligent reader in finding the bearings of those great subjects, national taxation and revenue. Some plain, clear statements by gentlemen whose views of a national economic policy are presented from the scientific standpoint, will serve a real educational purpose.

"It being generally conceded that Congress must cut off some existing sources of revenue, and reduce the surplus income, in what way should the reduction be made, and upon what governing considerations?

"Should it be attempted, by refunding or in some other way, to bring the public debt into such form as to permit the continuance of a policy of somewhat rapid payment, or should we adjust the revenues upon a plan that will allow nothing for debt payment beyond sinking-fund requirements?

"In a policy for the more immediate future should we contemplate the special encouragement of trade with Canada, Mexico, and the states of Central and South America, by means of a 'commercial union' or 'zollverein' arrangement, steamship subsidies, reciprocity treaties, or otherwise?

"What do you regard as the probable or proper future of the American protective system, and what would be the ideal sources of a national revenue?"

Several gentlemen from whom contributions were asked were unable for various reasons to comply. Because a "qualitative" rather than a "quantitative" analysis was sought, it was endeavored to secure expressions that would be representative; and while further extension of the inquiry might have obtained the opinions of as many more gentlemen equally entitled to speak for the economists of the United States, the tone of the collection would hardly have been altered.

The recent writer of an anonymous book on "Class Interests" has a suggestive chapter on the "Biases of Economical Teachers." Speaking of their teachings on the subject of "American protection," he says: "We think there are very many intelligent people with hearts aright who have not reflected sufficiently on the influences affecting their own minds in relation to class interests to realize why their sympathies incline to one view rather than to another.

Manly sympathies indeed they have, but these are often misdirected from perversion of judgment under the influence of bias." Perhaps the thoughtful reader of this collection of letters from "economical teachers" upon "American Protection" may detect here and there the unconscious working of class bias.

III.

It may not be out of order to say something briefly of the gentlemen whose contributions make up this volume. The productive activity of the colleges and universities has been already mentioned as the most noteworthy fact respecting recent American writing in the general domain of political and social science. And reference has also been made, as a part of the same striking tendency, to the growing intimacy between the universities and the administration of public affairs. With the assumption of an eminently practical and scientific cast, the economic study of the day is receiving a deference and attention from the public altogether unprecedented.

The consideration which General Francis A. Walker's important works on "Wages" and "Money" received upon their appearance a few years ago, and the recognition of his ability as a statistician and economist which his appointment as superintendent of the last federal census indicated, are no longer exceptional. Yet as President of the Massachusetts Institute of Technology, as President of the American Economic Association, as an author and scholar of worldwide repute, and as a practical man of affairs, Gen. Walker's influence is probably greater than that of any other American economist. His brief remarks in the following pages upon the surplus revenue crisis are full of weight.

Professor Richard T. Ely, of the Johns Hopkins University, is widely esteemed and read as an authority upon questions of labor, taxation, and national economics; and besides his better known writings he has lately issued a most instructive report upon systems and methods of State and municipal taxation, the outcome of his practical experience as a member of the tax commission of Maryland and of a board charged with the revision of the tax system of Baltimore.

Professor Henry C. Adams, lately of Cornell and now of Michigan University, discusses questions of American finance as a recognized authority. His treatise on "Public Debts" is perhaps the most important systematic work in the science of finance that has been accomplished by an American; and while it is theoretical in the sense that it discovers underlying principles and defines broad rules of action, it is practical in the sense that it deals with actual problems in such a way as to have influence in shaping the policies of government.

Professor Arthur T. Hadley, of Yale, who contributes to this collection a paper on subsidies as a means for the employment of surplus revenue, illustrates well the new relation of intimacy between the universities and public affairs. His book on "Railroad Transportation" was continually cited as high authority in the Congressional debates that preceded the enactment of the Inter-State Commerce law, and is a text-book in the hands alike of railroad officials and of State legislators. It is understood that Professor Hadley was proffered a place in the Inter-State Commerce Commission. His merits as a student of industrial society led to his appointment as labor commissioner of Connecticut, a post which he held for two years with rare ability.

Professor Robert Ellis Thompson, of the Wharton School of Finance and Economy at the University of Pennsylvania, represents an institution which has long given especial prominence to American history and economics, with a pronounced influence upon affairs of state. Professor Thompson is one of the foremost advocates of protection as a national economic policy. He is also a constant writer for the press, and an exponent of the views of those who urge "commercial union" between the United States and Canada and the policy of freer and more intimate trade relations throughout the western hemisphere.

As further instances of the new relation of political economists to public affairs it may be noted that Professor A. S. Bolles, recently a colleague of Professor Thompson, and well-known as the author of a "Financial History of the United States" and the editor of the "Banker's Magazine," has become the Commissioner of Labor Statistics for the State of Pennsylvania; and that the retention of the Philadelphia Gas Works as public property is attributed in large part to the personal activity of Professor E. J. James, another colleague of Professor Thompson, and to the influence of his convincing monograph on the "Relation of the Modern Municipality to the Gas Supply."

The Columbia College (New York) School of Political Science is represented in these pages by its teachers of political economy, Professor Richmond M. Smith and his colleague Professor Edwin R. A. Seligman, both of whom are economic writers of great force and keen perception, whose work is notable at once for its scholarly qualities and its practical spirit and direction, as witness Professor Seligman's admirable book entitled "Railway Tariffs and the Inter-State Commerce Law," and Professor Smith's current writing on the control of immigration.

Political economy at Harvard University has

attained a constantly growing prominence under the enthusiasm and activity of Professors Dunbar, Laughlin and Taussig. Professor J. Laurence Laughlin, who contributes to the present collection a paper on the tariff and wages, is the author of an important historical and critical work on "Bimetallism in the United States," and has obtained rank as an authority on currency questions and other problems of national economics, while deservedly holding a high place as a writer in the general science of political economy.

Professor John B. Clark of Smith College (Northampton, Massachusetts), who writes a paper on "The Certainties of the Tariff Question," has reflected much credit upon the study of political economy in America by his elucidation of principles in the light of such modern facts as great combinations of capital, labor organizations, enlarged governmental activity, etc.,—a line of fundamental study of exceeding importance as a pre-requisite to intelligent legislation.

Professor Anson D. Morse, of Amherst College, is well known as a student and writer in the fields of American history and political science.

Professor Woodrow Wilson, of the Bryn Mawr College, the author of "Congressional Government," is recognized as one of the keenest and most brilliant of all the writers who have undertaken the critical discussion of our constitutional machinery and administrative method.

Professor William W. Folwell, of the University of Minnesota, who contributes a remarkably clear elucidation of the position and character of the tariff question in a general scheme of economics, is one of the most accomplished, most experienced and most truly representative of American economists.

Professor Jesse Macy, of Iowa College, has rendered a great service to education and citizenship by his successful efforts to promote under proper methods the study of civil government and of the elements of political science in the common schools of America; and in his text-book "Our Government" he has given the best and fullest view ever presented of our hierarchy of institutions, beginning with the primary political groups, the townships, etc., and ascending finally to the organs of the national administration.

Professor James H. Canfield, of the University of Kansas, is widely known among American educators, and is specially commended as a university professor who keeps the work of his department of history and political science in close sympathy and relationship with the history-making activity of the surrounding life.

Chancellor Irving J. Manatt, the head of the University of Nebraska, though disavowing all claim to speak as a specialist, is an excellent representative of the men of varied scholarship and wide observation, who stand as leaders in American education.

Among the young men of rising reputation who are finding places in college chairs of political science, are Professors Arthur Yager and Edward W. Bemis. Dr. Yager, of the Georgetown (Kentucky) College, has written ably upon American war financiering; and Dr. Bemis, now of the Vanderbilt University (Tennessee), has published valuable monographs upon industrial cooperation and other phases of the the labor question.

Of the work as an industrial statistician of Hon. Carroll D. Wright, the United States Commissioner of Labor, and long the Chief of the Massachusetts Bureau of Statistics of Labor, it would be almost superfluous to speak. His timely and impartial investigations have thrown floods of light upon obscure and difficult problems, and have furnished a safe guide for much legislation that otherwise must have proceeded blindly and uncertainly. His proposal in these pages of a scientific basis for tariff legislation is worthy of the most serious consideration.

In the recent movement which has given the study of political science so remarkable an impetus in this country, history and economics have been closely allied,—so closely, indeed, that their teaching and investigation have been inseparably blended. And nothing could be more fortunate for both than this alliance. As Professor Herbert B. Adams truly says, in his recent comprehensive work on the "The Study of History in American Colleges and Universities," while discussing the historical method in economics,—"The two subjects are naturally allied, and can never be absolutely separated in American university life with its present tendencies. Without indulging extreme or one-sided views, the writer believes it the destiny of history to become more economic, and of economics to become more historical in both object and method. History has too long neglected the ways and means, the practical side of social and political life, and economics have too long neglected the simple facts."

It is cordially admitted on all sides that nothing else has done so much to give impulse to the investigation under American college and university auspices of our past and present institutional and economic life, as the publication of the "Johns Hopkins University Studies in Historical and Political Science," now in their sixth annual series under the editorship of their originator Professor Adams. From the impetus which must be ascribed in no small part to these publications sprang the American Historical and the American Economic Associations, the two being composed very largely of the same membership. These societies show remarkable vigor, and are more successful in fostering original and scientific research than the most sanguine of their founders had dared to expect. Both of them issue publications in regular monographic series.

As further welcome results of the new impulse have been founded two quarterly reviews, one at Columbia and the other at Harvard, both of which have sprung at once into mature existence and taken rank among the most important journals of their character in the world. The "Political Science Quarterly," edited by the faculty of political science of Columbia College, now beginning its third year, is "a review devoted to the historical, statistical, and comparative study of politics, economics, and public law." The "Quarterly Journal of Economics," under the auspices of Harvard University, now about completing its second volume, is devoted to the discussion by the best economic writers and investigators of the most practical problems of the day. At the University of Pennsylvania, also, a series of publications in the line of economics and public law has been begun under the editorship of Professor E. J. James. Through these various avenues of publication there has appeared within the last half decade an aggregate mass of economic literature possessing extraordinary variety, permanent importance, and current practical value of the highest order.

The editor of this volume scarcely need make apology for having spoken thus at length, although necessarily in a general and incomplete way, of the new movement in the American study of political economy, of its *personnel*, its methods, and its already visible results. It may be further unnecessary to say that the editor, himself so situated as to be free from the possibility of "the biases of economical teachers," stands committed neither to the views of individual contributors, nor to what may be regarded as the prevailing tone of the contributions as a whole, upon national revenue questions. The collection of views is published simply for what it may be worth for the elucidation of practical questions of great moment, and for the disclosure of the present mental attitude of the schools towards national policies and problems of statesmanship.

ALBERT SHAW.

PROTECTIVE TARIFFS AS A QUESTION OF NATIONAL ECONOMY.

By Professor William W. Folwell, of the University of Minnesota.

There is but one live question in general politics at the present moment. The revenue system of the general government had been organized upon the expectation that the income would for an indefinite period be exhausted in liquidating the war debt. By a mistake in estimating the paying ability of the nation, a thousand millions of that debt were put into "long bonds," to mature, one-fourth in 1891, the remainder in 1907. An act of 1881 authorized the Secretary of the Treasury to devote any surplus of funds to the purchase of any bonds which holders might please to offer. Opinions differ as to whether this act was or was not of mere temporary force; the present administration chose to give it the construction of a temporary provision, whose authority has been exhausted. In consequence, there soon appeared masses of unusable money in the vaults of the treasury. The 49th Congress was aware of this, but neglected to give any definite construction to the Act of 1881, and this laches apparently sustained the construction of the administration. The surplus grew and still continues to swell, and the prospect now is that the end of the present fiscal year will find the treasury in possession of a hundred and forty millions of which it can make no use, unless the legislature in the meantime provides for its disposition.

This fact is an alarming one. It is a maxim universally accepted that the taxing power should never be exercised so as to allow a government to take out and keep out of the pockets of the people, more money than the uses of the government require. Excessive revenue tempts to unusual and extravagant expenditure, by which individuals, classes or localities unjustly may profit.

The President had a right to be alarmed, and it was his duty to lay the dangerous condition of the finances before Congress. It is, however, a question whether the situation was so desperate as to justify the executive in departing from long and well established usage in the composition of the annual message. It was probably not necessary, in order to arouse sleeping Senators and drowsy representatives, that a campaign document be flung in the face of the country.

And such a document the annual message of the President to the first session of the 50th Congress has proved to be, whether so intended or not. The President's text was the treasury surplus; his sermon was upon the wicked tariff tax, and his outpouring was so impassioned that a suspicion has naturally arisen that it was not, after all, the surplus itself which lay so heavy on the Presidential heart.

The head of the State has made the tariff question the issue of the campaign which is now opening. It is one worthy the mettle of statesmen and of great parties. The clans are already gathering and are taking up their positions in the opposing lines of battle. In such crises issues have to be simplified; contestants must be furnished with short and easy formulas; argument gives place to noisy iteration. Extreme statements answer these ends better than moderate ones, which need to be guarded and limited.

We are assured by the Free Traders that the non-manufacturing producers of the country are now ground into the dust by the taxes laid on them for the benefit of manufacturers. High nominal wages are reduced to low real wages by taxes put upon articles of general use and consumption.

Protectionists reply that the removal of existing duties will close the factories and drive the operatives out to the fields to divide the wages of farm laborers. Wages, they say, now kept up by artificial diversification of industry, will drop to some unknown level, while British traders engrossing our markets will revel in unlimited profits drawn from our helpless people.

If it might be possible amid the thunder of the captains and the shouting to gain a moment's quiet and a clear view of the situation of things, an unprejudiced observer might suggest to the combatants some principles which might mitigate the conflict and establish a *modus vivendi* at its close.

The tariff question is not one of political economy, as commonly understood and taught in the schools. That science, as imported from England and treated by American writers, discusses the economic functions and relations of individual men socially related. Laying down a body of guiding postulates, such as self-interest, economic freedom, the principle of parsimony, this science proceeds to derive such conclusions as seem to be warranted by the canons of deductive logic. No fault is to be found with so noble and useful a science. The fault lies with those teachers who fail to observe and to teach that political economy does not cover the whole field of economics.

Men can not exist as individuals, nor do they now exist in mere social groups. The SOCIETAS of the barbarian long since gave place to the CIVITAS of the civilized man. The law of the land long ago took the place of the local and uncertain law of the clan or the tribe. The State has made government permanent, impartial, supreme, both necessary and possible. Law has been crystallized out of custom, concessions have blossomed into rights, justice has replaced the *lex talionis*, the government of the State is the great agency of justice, the guarantor of rights, the author of law.

Modern civilized men therefore do not live but in States having each its ascertained boundaries, its system of public justice, its armed force, its official language, its traditions and history, giving rise to a body of sentiments indicated by the word PATRIOTISM. These great civic communities have their own peculiar economic interests as well as their own political institutions. It is the economic relations of States which the political economy of the schools has belittled or altogether ignored. We must not at this point, however, neglect to take into account a respectable body of American writers who, observing with impatience this narrowness of the orthodox economists in ignoring the State, have leapt to the opposite extreme and denied the name of science to the traditional political economy. Such is the ground taken in a well-known text-book entitled "Social Science and National Economy." There is no occasion to go to such extremes. The comprehending truth lies in the middle ground. There are two great divisions of the economic field, the one to which the name Political Economy has by long usage become attached, the other which is probably to be known by the title National Economy. Under this title of national economy may be assembled a large mass of phenomena which are capable not merely of enumeration, but of arrangement into an orderly system of filiation. There is a public economy of population, property, money and banks, trade and transportation, labor, health and morals, just as there is a private economy of wealth, capital, division of labor, rent, profit and value.

The tariff question is a question of national economy. It is useless and impracticable to object here with the old story of the French merchants and their phrase, "*laisser aller, laisser passer.*" The government can not let alone. The State has economic interests which must be managed by the government as the agent of the collective people. The moment the government declares by statute what shall be tender in payment of debt, that moment she is stirring in every family dinner pot. Taxation involves the disclosure of every man's private affairs and thrusts official hands into private pockets. While the schools are faithfully inculcating "*laisser faire,*" the interference of government in finance, education, railways, labor, has been steadily increasing for a generation. On the postoffice, the public school system, the powers reposed in boards of health, the State Socialists found their expectations of government custody and management of all means of production, land, machines, raw materials. Government cannot let alone, and the most troublesome problem of the future economist is to place the proper limits to public economy.

· Further, the economic agency of government becomes indispensable when the economic interests and enterprises of other states come into collision with those of our own. The great civilized states have not, according to a convenient fiction of writers, been developed in different climatic zones, thus ensuring a territorial division of labor and an impossibility of competition in like industries. Most civilized peoples both produce and consume the same cereals, domestic animals, fruits and fabrics; hence industrial and commercial complications which the State cannot ignore. States exist, furthermore, in many stages of economic developement. The few nations which have put steam and electricity into common use, have placed themselves a century in advance of others. Some peoples have voluntarily and purposely put themselves under a course of industrial training and education, while others are still content with accidental and fortuitous culture. There are nations which have provided themselves with a machinery of banks and exchange rendering vast operations easy to them, but which are utterly beyond the power of peoples not so furnished. A given state must, then, regulate its economic affairs according to its own economic status as compared with that of its neighbors. Like a wise man, a state will not suffer its whole wealth to be exhausted by foreigners because it is a good thing in general to contribute to the needy. Each state must then apply the general maxims of national economy to its own exigencies and circumstances.

The tariff question as it is now before us is a question of American public economy, and it is a double question; involving, (1) a public policy of trade and industry, and (2) a question of taxation.

It may be taken as axiomatic that as long as nations continue to exist, they will provide for themselves those things which are necessary to national existence; such as arms and ammunition, fortifications, ships of war, and all the supplies needful for the support of navies and armies, iron and steel, leather, cloth, etc., etc.; further, each nation will of course, seek to be furnished on its own ground with all things essential to the life of its people, so that they may not be endangered by hostile blockades and embargoes, or the failure of harvests or stoppage of production in other lands. To secure these ends, modern governments in extreme cases enter themselves on the field of production, and in their own shops and factories manufacture the weapons and fabrics deemed to be essential. The German empire establishes horse-farms to ensure the supply of cavalry horses. In some cases, monopolies have been granted to individuals as a stimulus to the certain production of essential articles. Governments also offer bounties for the production of goods the manufacture of which can not be expected to yield an average rate of profit, such goods being regarded as essential to the independence of the people, and this brings in another consideration. Modern states are not content merely to secure to themselves a military independence; they aspire to be industrially and commercially free. The modern state is not merely a political state; it is an industrial state. No enlightened people can be content to be in the rear of the general line of industrial progress, diversifying its employments, opening its mines and deposits, extending its lines of communication, and entering the markets of the world with the finished products of its own raw materials. Hamilton, with his usual intuition, has suggested that a people who neglect manufactures thereby fail to avail themselves of the forces and properties of nature. The generative power of nature appears, of course, in agriculture; but its scope is limited, at least in the present state of that art, while there is hardly any assignable limit to the amount of force which machines cannot educe and convert into work.

The public policy of a modern state must embrace the industrial interests of the people. American public economy will provide not merely for the military and industrial independence but for the general industrial advance of the nation, to keep that abreast of the general progress of other industrial states.

The possible means and ways by which this policy may be carried out are various, but in the present article of our national development and in the present political crisis there is but one system which can demand attention. Here we reach the other phase of the tariff question,—that of taxation.

We are in a certain historical situation. The revolutionary government having no revenue system, carried on its operations by means of borrowed money and small and occasional contributions by the states. The confederation was, according to its articles, to receive "quotas" of money from the several states, proportioned to the extent of improved lands. This plan proved unworkable, and when that unfortunate government could no longer borrow of its creditors to pay their interest, its fate was sealed. The Confederation Congress in April, 1783, proposed to the states an amendment to the articles which should empower the United States to raise revenue by duties on imports, that is to say, by specific duties on liquors, teas, coffees, sugars and a few other articles, and a "horizontal" ad valorem duty on all other imported goods. This amendment never received the approval of the states so as to become a part of the constitution.

The new house of representatives was hardly organized under the constitution of 1787, before Madison brought in a bill to establish the proposed tariff of 1783. The bill, considerably amended, became a law July 4th, 1789. No other course was at the time possible. The treasury was empty, it could not pay the per diem of the members of Congress. There was no machinery for collecting revenue directly from the people, and the people had not been accustomed to taxation for that vague and distant thing known as the United States Government. The senators and representatives could from the windows of their chambers see vessels sailing up New York Bay laden with costly freights from beyond seas. On these a few customs officials could at once levy the charges which would pay their salaries and put in motion all the springs of the new government. Under the circumstances no other course was open to the first Congress. Two years later Hamilton at the request of Congress drew up his well known "report on manufactures." The time, the place, the traditions of a former and the fashion of his own age, conspired to give Hamilton's treatise a force against which opposition was impossible. Indeed even at this time, Hamilton seems to have so covered the ground and exhausted arguments as to leave no room for novelty to his successors on his side of the question. The tariff of 1792 conformed in essentials to Hamilton's suggestions, and fixed the protective policy on the country for an indefinite time. We are now nearing the close of a century during which that policy has been steadily maintained. No serious proposition has been made to abandon the system of indirect taxation for the support and uses of the general government. It is American policy to raise moneys by import duties so adjusted as to discriminate favorably to American industry and to insure the production, within the limits of our own territory, of all the things needful to industrial independence and to the industrial advancement of the collective people. In this historical situation there is no room for the doctrinaire on either side of the question. The national economist, in particular, has no right to dogmatize. His business is to deal with things as they are in his day, his maxims are always to be adjusted to the circumstances of his age, his practical measures should be adapted to the situation of the hour. Because a certain industry has needed the fostering care of government in one decade it does not follow that it should not at length go alone. Because the country has grown steadily in wealth and power under a protective policy, it does not follow that protection has been the sole cause of prosperity. Economists of all sorts are constantly in danger of singling out some part of a compound cause, and treating that element as if it were the only efficient one, all others being merely contributory.

If these prologomena to the consideration of the tariff question, now before the country, and which every citizen has got to face on the calends of November, shall assist somewhat in simplifying and elucidating that question, I shall be glad to have contributed them.

WILLIAM W. FOLWELL.

SURPLUS FINANCIERING.

By Professor Henry C. Adams, of the University of Michigan.

Upon one point, at least, there can be no difference of opinion with regard to the present financial situation of the United States. It is universally agreed that the federal government must spend, in some manner, all the moneys collected in the form of taxes. This necessity is imposed upon it by the fact that trade would be impeded were any considerable part of the accustomed amount of money withdrawn from circulation. There is now about $1,600,000,000 of money in circulation. Should the revenue laws remain unchanged, and no appropriations more than ordinarily extravagant be made by Congress at the present session, the surplus revenue for the coming year will probably amount to $125,000,000, or about one-twelfth of the total circulation. Now it is mere confession of ignorance to say that a contraction of currency equal to one-twelfth of its amount within a year can do no harm to trade. It would tend to bring about a stringent money market, and would probably precipitate a commercial crisis. Or should these evils be obviated by extraordinary exertions on the part of the banks, it would yet introduce into trade an element of uncertainty, and rest like a dead weight upon all business enterprises.

The fact thus disclosed, that the government cannot hoard its surplus funds, suggests the true statement of the financial problem. The maintenance of surplus revenue means the continuance of surplus expenditures; and the question at issue is :— Shall Congress open up new avenues for the disbursement of its excessive income, or shall it reduce the income by reducing taxes ? Turning our attention for the present to the first alternative, there are three suggestions: First, the money may be applied to continue the extinction of the debt ; second, it may be applied to new and unusual appropriations ; third, it may be disbursed to the states for the purpose of reducing state taxes.

Can the surplus be judiciously used in paying the debt ?

Until within a few months, no embarrassment has arisen on account of the surplus, because all money not otherwise appropriated was easily returned to circulation by applying it to the redemption of the public debt. This was possible because a considerable portion of the debt was redeemable at the pleasure of the government, and on this account could be paid at par ;

but since all matured debt has now been redeemed, if the government still desires to continue the expungement of its obligations, it will be obliged to buy them in open market. No objection can be urged against such a plan, provided speculative prices are not paid for bonds purchased; but speculative prices will undoubtedly be paid if the government relies upon this avenue of expenditure for returning all surplus revenue to circulation. Bondholders could ask for no better chance to squeeze the Treasury. The demand for bonds would be constant and imperative, while their supply would be limited and constantly decreasing. Under such conditions a bond would stand at premium even though it paid no interest whatever. We conclude, then, that purchase of bonds would be a piece of extravagance.

It has been suggested that this difficulty could be overcome by means of a refunding operation, the object of which should be to purchase from creditors the liberty of paying the principal of the bonds before maturity and the accruing interest before it becomes due. It is probable the price demanded for such liberty would be high, but it would surely amount to less than the speculative premiums which the government would be obliged to pay if it should adopt the policy of redemption by purchase. The reason for this conclusion is that the government can now get better terms as to the conditions of future payment than if it wait until cornered on the market. Still, a refunding operation would not solve the question of surplus revenue. The argument in its favor is that money will be saved by means of it, not that it will provide an avenue of unlimited expenditure. It is probable that the right to appropriate more than $75,000,000 or $80,000,000 a year to the service of debt could not be secured from creditors on advantageous terms. But the expenditure for the debt at the present time, if we include only accruing interest and sinking fund dues, is $85,000,000. We must, therefore, unless we are willing to approve of recklessness and extravagance in the continued payment of the debt, look in some other direction for relief from surplus revenue.*

Shall the surplus be returned to circulation by means of extraordinary expenditures?

No one can for a moment doubt the ability of Congress to get rid of the money. The pension agents would gladly give suggestions. The cigar-makers' union have kindly expressed their willingness to take several millions for the purpose of establishing a co-operative manufactory embracing all the cigar-makers in the United States. Or, if really hard pressed, possibly the

---

*In the December (1887) number of the *Forum*, I endeavored to explain the principles on which a refunding operation might be carried through.

plan of a Michigan man might commend itself, that the Federal Government should build a town hall in every town of over ten thousand inhabitants, not because a hall is needed for any federal purpose, but to be a silent witness to the authority of the central government. These are but samples of the many proposals which will surely present themselves so long as money continues to trickle down the sides of an over-flowing treasury. That the employment of the taxing power for such ends is contrary to established principles of government can not be called in question. That a lavish and unnecessary expenditure of public funds is the first step to political corruption is equally beyond controversy. Yet who, knowing the workings of popular government, can believe that Congress will have the wisdom and stamina for withstanding popular clamor, so long as it has at command the material means of satisfying clamor. Surplus revenue will inevitably become a corruption fund for party purposes.

It is not, however, necessary to discuss this question on the assumption that Congress will make an unwise disposal of the surplus. There are many ways in which the money might be invested to the advantage of the public. The Blair educational bill has much in its favor. A comprehensive system of public forestry would add to national wealth. It might be opportune to purchase the telegraph property. And yet for Congress to take steps in any of these directions *before it has passed laws reducing taxes*, would place popular government in America in greater jeopardy than a corrupt use of public funds. Mr. Sherman in his late manifesto is chargeable with narrowness of view when he says that the surplus is the occasion of no danger because of the many ways in which the money may be spent. He overlooks entirely the constitutional bearings of the question. In theory, government in this country finds the limits of its authority in the grants of specific powers; in fact no limits can be placed upon the encroachments of a government having control over surplus funds. In theory, the guarantee of personal liberty lies in the political responsibility of officers of state; in fact, the guarantee amounts to nothing, when the treasury is full and officers are not dependent upon the continuous consent of the people for the disbursement of funds. In theory, the unity of this vast country is maintained by the observance of a just balance of authority between the states and the federal government; in fact, that balance is seriously threatened, if not already destroyed, by the financial preponderance of the federal treasury over the State treasuries. Such tendencies as these are difficult to trace, but that they should be ignored by the men who are asking to be entrusted with the political guidance of this great country is beyond excuse.

Shall the surplus revenue be distributed to the States?

They who urge this plan hope it will commend itself to the voters of the several States because it promises reduction of State taxation. The arguments against this scheme are not financial; they are political and constitutional. The continuous distribution of money by the federal government would surely result in the absolute subjection of the States to federal authority. It is a scheme which looks toward imperialism, and is, therefore, dangerous to republican government. Clearness in accounts, simplicity in methods of procedure, and definitely limited powers, are essential to the success of popular government. They are in large measure secured by the maintenance of independent sources of revenue, and it is now proposed to abandon them for the uncertain benefits of a slight reduction in local taxes. Political charlatans alone will reap the advantages of so pernicious choice. Although such a line of thought is too extended for complete presentation in a short paper, I can not forego this opportunity of calling attention to one fact which seems to have been thus far overlooked in the present controversy. They make a mistaken appeal to history who urge the distribution of the surplus in 1837 as a precedent for the plan now before the country. For in the first place the distribution of 1837 was a deposit of federal funds with the States, thus evading one of the constitutional objections which would otherwise have proven fatal to it. But of more importance than this, it was the deposit of money which happened to be left over after paying the public debt, and after a law reducing the revenue that had been put into operation. It did not contemplate that federal taxes should be made a constant source of revenue to the States. Were the present scheme of distribution brought forward under the same conditions, that is to say, should Congress first reduce federal revenue to federal needs, and then propose laws for getting rid in a judicious manner of funds which must come in before the reduction of taxes become effective, the criticisms which we have urged would be set one side. The Blair bill might then be considered in view of its relation to the interests of education alone. Or money might be given to the States for the purpose of establishing a general system of forestry. The financial transaction between the central government and the States would not establish a permanent relation between them, but be temporary in its nature because the surplus itself would soon pass away. Under such conditions the pernicious constitutional tendencies of which we have spoken would not show themselves.

The conclusion from the foregoing suggestions is plain. It is not safe for the United States to consider any question of expenditure whatever until the laws pertaining to federal revenue are radically modified. It is dangerous even to enter upon a discussion of other questions until this necessary step is taken.

Reduction of Revenue.

But how may the revenue be reduced? Upon this point I shall merely give my own views without discussion. In my opinion the first step toward a reduction of the revenue should be the extension of the free list until it includes all crude materials for manufacture. This would take away the necessity for protective duties on many manufactured products, and would permit mineral lands and lumber lands to fall to their true commercial values independently of protective duties. The second step toward a reduction of revenue should be the reduction of the tax on whisky and tobacco until the rate imposed shall stand considerably below the maximum revenue rate. The reason for maintaining these taxes is the general belief that the tax lessens the consumption of the commodities named. I confess myself to be a little skeptical respecting the ability of Congress to influence greatly the morals of the people by means of fiscal machinery. At least the fiscal argument is strongly in favor of reduction. A sound revenue system should be elastic; otherwise it can not be employed with advantage in times of emergency. But no revenue system is elastic unless the rates ordinarily charged are below the maximum revenue rate. The machinery of internal revenue should be maintained because its existence is indispensable in time of war, but in ordinary times it should be run at a low rate of speed or its usefulness in an emergency will be greatly impaired. It is strange that in the discussion of a financial question this most important financial consideration is kept in the background. The third step in the reduction of revenue should be the gradual reduction of customs duties on manufactured goods until they, too, shall stand below the maximum revenue rate. The financial argument for this is the same as the argument just given. A sound fiscal system must be elastic, and elasticity is impossible so long as taxes are above the maximum revenue rate. Protectionists urge that this step will destroy American industry. If this be true, it of course cannot be defended. But it is difficult for me to understand how one can hold such an opinion if he will read the list of manufacturing industries given in the tenth census, and ask how many of them would flourish in the face of foreign competition, *provided* they had free access to raw material. At least, such a study, and not a theory, is the basis of my opinion. "It is a *condition* which confronts us—not a theory."

The two thoughts which appear to be most prominent in the foregoing discussion are the following: First, the present financial situation is one that cannot continue without endangering the permanency of the form of government in which we profess to believe. The financial question is at bottom a question of constitutional tendencies. Second, in the reform of the revenue laws we are in danger of losing sight of the demands of a sound financial system. Congress would make more rapid headway, and proceed with greater safety to all interests concerned, if it should give some little attention to the requirements of a sound fiscal system, and put more confidence in the people to take care of the industries and the morals of the country.

HENRY C. ADAMS.

THE TARIFF AND TRUSTS — EXPENDITURES FOR INTERNAL IMPROVEMENTS.

By Professor Richard T. Ely, of the Johns Hopkins University.

I must frankly confess to you* that your circular letter is the most difficult letter to answer which I ever received. Your questions are far-reaching in their scope, and it would be necessary to write a large book to give anything approaching an adequate reply. It is undoubtedly a good thing to compare conclusions of specialists, but to state conclusions without any explanation of the methods whereby one arrives at those conclusions is apt to lead to serious misapprehension.

I must acknowledge that the changed circumstances of our time have driven me farther and farther away from any affection which I ever entertained for protectionism. The fact cannot be disguised that our protective tariff has been dreadfully abused. Its design was to shut off foreign competition altogether or to weaken its force, but not to prevent competition among domestic producers. Within a few years, however, home manufacturers, seeing foreign com-

---

*Dr. Ely's paper was written in the form of a letter to the editor.

petition excluded, have availed themselves of this circumstance to form trusts and combinations, whereby all competition has been excluded, all producers have been placed at the mercy of a ring, and those who have dared oppose them have been crushed by a tyranny in comparison with which the alleged tyranny of trades-unions sinks into insignificance. While profits of employers in the ring have been raised by this process enormously, workingmen, instead of finding their wages increased, have been entirely thrown out of employment, for when factories and shops are closed by these combinations no provision is ever made for the workingmen who in them formerly gained a livelihood. To talk about the benefits of protection to labor becomes under such circumstances a hollow mockery; especially so since evidence is not wanting to show that these huge monopolies propose to turn their immense power against all combinations of workingmen and crush them just as they have the independent producers. The fact is not to be gainsaid that trusts and combinations among producers are socialistic in character. They stand for the only real live and dangerous socialism which to-day exists, and their spread is greeted by scholarly socialists with unmingled satisfaction. What the socialists want is absolute concentration—concentration of all production under a single authority. *We may define socialism as an unlimited trust.* Socialists believe that by spontaneous processes as seen in modern combinations all production will some day be concentrated in a single management, when it will only be necessary to change the purpose of the management to inaugurate the reign of socialism. SOCIALISM I WILL DEFINE, THEN, AS THE EXCLUSIVE MANAGEMENT OF ALL PRODUCTION AND DISTRIBUTION BY A SINGLE TRUST ON BEHALF OF THE PEOPLE. Those who believe in competitive methods, or who even believe as I do, that the legitimate sphere of competition is a very large one, including by far the greater part of our industrial life, must look with alarm upon the modern trust, and must favor the removal of the protective tariff behind which it has intrenched itself.

The argument for protection to young industries may, under certain circumstances of time and place, have some force, and I am not prepared to admit that in no country should I ever favor protection. I do not call myself either a protectionist or a free trader so far as theory goes. I hardly think a universal law can in this matter be laid down. In the United States, at the present time, I am, so far as our own policy is concerned, a free trader. I would not introduce free trade to-day nor to-morrow; but with adequate regard for vested interests, I would gradually approach free trade. Is it not ridiculous to protect the strong against the weak? Yet that is what we are doing. We are becoming not merely the strongest but by far the strongest industrial nation on the face of the globe, and our industries need no protection.

Our farmers and our laborers gain no advantage whatever from protection. The market of the farmer is restricted. He sends his wheat to Liverpool, but in Liverpool he may not purchase in exchange those things which he needs, for we make it impossible by taxes on imported commodities. He must buy in New York and pay larger prices to men who have no more affection for him than his Liverpool customers. The plea is urged that a diversified industry is needed. No doubt the farmer is interested in a diversified industry, but that will come of itself. We have superior facilities for a vast number of industries, and I do not believe that any great industry would be completely ruined should free trade be introduced in the United States to-day. Many engaged in the production of iron and steel might be obliged to close their establishments, but it would be found that the superior facilities of some would enable them to continue. It is asked, What would those do who would be thrown out of work should we import things now produced at home? Manifestly, it is impossible to import commodities unless we export commodities in return. Foreigners will not send us goods unless we give them goods in exchange. Those who are manufacturing things which, under a system of free trade, we would import, would find an occupation in producing goods for exportation. Free trade, or perhaps I ought to say freer trade, would bring about a better international division of labor. We would produce those things for which we have special gifts, as would foreign countries, and thus the products of labor and capital would, to the benefit of all, improve both quantitatively and qualitatively.

If the advance towards free trade is made without due regard to existing conditions, the result will be the bankruptcy of many large manufacturers; and it is true that you cannot affect one industrial interest adversely without touching all others. Our economic life is an organism, and every part of it is connected with every other part. I have always favored the proposition of Mr. Hugh McCulloch, our former secretary of the treasury, that a commission of impartial, fair-minded men, extremists neither in the interests of free trade nor in the direction of protection, be appointed to investigate the condition of our industries, and on the basis of their investigation to report a tariff bill. The unsatisfactory experience of the country with the tariff commissioners of 1882 proves nothing. That commission was appointed, not to bring in an important report, but a report in favor of protection. The nature of its report was avowedly known from the start, and it was not based on the results of investigation. It seems to me that at the present time a more satisfactory commission could be appointed. It ought to include both scholars and business men. A business man like Hon. Abram S. Hewitt, and scholars like Professors Taussig and E. J. James, differing in views, yet both inclined to be fair-minded, would be admirable members of a tariff commission.

My general ideas in regard to tariff reform are in favor of a simplification of administration by a substitution of specific for ad valorem duties in every practicable instance, and as large an extension of the free list as possible. Every time an article is added to the free list one temptation to political corruption and "government by special interests" is removed.

I am in favor of reducing the debt by bond purchases whenever favorable opportunity offers, and also in favor of a *protective expenditure of the surplus*. There is an opportunity for the advantageous expenditure of the existing surplus, and the free traders do not do themselves credit by their demagogical objections to every legitimate plan for the use of the national surplus. Their aim is, of course, to force the tariff question on the country by the accumulation of a surplus, and they are too often willing to see a waste of national resources rather than consent to the wise expenditure of public money. I doubt, however, whether they strengthen themselves thereby. The practical outcome of this attitude is after all not economy, but a wasteful and disadvantageous expenditure of money in ways calculated to catch votes, as seen in most objectionable pension bills.

The newspaper outcry about river and harbor bills is largely to be explained in this way—partially also by the inspiration of railroad men, who, above all things, do not want to see any improvement in our natural and artificial waterways.

The amount of lying done about the character of appropriations for the improvement of rivers and harbors is something astounding. Conversation with any intelligent and honest man who knows anything about the internal improvements going on under the supervision of the federal government will show one that large appropriations, larger than any we have had, are really needed, will show one that money so spent would yield enormous returns to the people of the United States. My attention was first called to the true nature of newspaper criticisms of river and harbor bills by a United States engineer who in character and intelligence ranks among the highest in the service. His name is well known, but it may be better, on account of his official position, not to mention it in this place. Since that time, all that I have observed has confirmed the statements of this engineer. A year ago this last winter, I visited Charleston, S. C., and Savannah, Ga., and found a considerable portion of the appropriations for those important harbors wasted on account of their insufficiency. Let us suppose that $400,000 is needed at once for the improvement of a harbor, and $200,000 is appropriated. It will often be necessary to suspend work until more is appropriated, and in the meantime the sea will destroy a part of what has been done. This is a sample of the penny-wise, pound-foolish policy of Congress. Our Baltimore appropriations are quite insufficient. Although a believer in tariff reform, I quite agree with these sensible remarks quoted from the " Real Estate Record and Builders Guide " of New York for March 31, 1888 : " Ours is an immense country, with innumerable waterways and harbors, or lake and ocean fronts. The growth of our enormous internal commerce calls for the improvement of these waterways and harbors, and the amount of work to be done is naturally very great. The local government engineers state officially that we ought to expend one hundred and sixty millions per annum for some years, in order to give the needed facilities to the internal commerce of the country. Knowing how impossible it would be to get Congress to sanction so large a sum, the chief of the government engineers asks for only forty millions. * * The House Committee has introduced a bill asking for less than twenty millions. * * The inadequacy of the proposed expenditures is shown in the fact that the harbor of New York gets only $200,000, when to deepen the channel in the lower bay properly would cost nearly $4,000,000. $150,000 is given to the Harlem River improvement, when the total cost of the work will be nearly $2,000,000. * * * Quite a large sum is appropriated for the lower Mississippi, not one tenth enough, however, to insure against inundations due to any exceptional rise in the river. * * If we are as niggardly in the future as in the past, the recent appalling catastrophe due to the breaking of the banks of the Yellow River in China will be repeated in our Mississippi Valley. A large sum is also appropriated to the Sault Ste. Marie Ship Canal, through which more tonnage will pass than through the Suez Canal. The appropriations should have been five millions for this work, instead of less than one million.

"But the newspapers have commenced to clamor against the new River and Harbor bill. It does look so honest to object to the spending of money by the government. A thievish pension bill gets no such criticism, though it is money worse than wasted. In the bill so unjustly vetoed by President Arthur, there was an appropriation for a locality called Cheesequakes, and how the wits of the press did play upon that name to cast odium upon the bill, of which nine-tenths of the appropriation were for objects of undoubted merit! In the bill now before the House it is proposed to deepen the Wing Wang River in Oregon. What a chance is here for the newspaper humorists! It is very probable that this tremendous press opposition to waterway improvements is really inspired by the great railway corporations, who naturally want to have the whole carrying trade of the country at their mercy."

While some of the money appropriated may be wasted—perfection is not possible in human affairs—by far the greater portion of the money is well spent, and it is to be hoped that we may some day have a Congress with back-bone enough to withstand newspaper clamor, and make adequate appropriations for rivers and harbors and defences of our sea coast cities; also for a few great canals.

The clamor about public buildings is equally senseless. Money worth to the United States is less than three per cent per annum. Now, wherever government spends $1,000 for rent, it would save money to invest $25,000 in a building. Many cities have no federal building, and they could with advantage be supplied with one. I would gladly see the amount of rent paid by the government diminished, and then in time of emergency we would derive advantage from the decrease in regular, ordinary expenditures.

I would gladly see the property of existing telegraph companies purchased by the federal government. It is a disgrace that we alone of civilized nations have no public telegraph service, and that we are obliged to put up with our present abominably inefficient and expensive private monopoly.

Heartily as I am in favor of tariff reform, I would gladly see the revenues remain as large as at present, and a proper, that is to say, a productive expenditure of revenues. Among these expenditures, in addition to those named, I would include some such plan of refunding the debt as that so ably advocated by Professor Henry C. Adams in his article in the "Forum" for December, 1887. The main feature of the article was the separation of interest from the principal of debt, the capitalization of the interest and its prepayment. The advantage to be derived from this plan by the government, and the inducement properly to be offered bond-holders, are satisfactorily described in the article.

I am in favor of an extension of commercial relations, and would gladly see a satisfactory scheme for a zoll-verein or commercial union for all of North and South America, devised and put in execution.

The main features of an ideal system of national revenues would, in my opinion, be these: Taxes laid on a few imported commodities for the sake of revenue; an internal revenue system laying taxes on a few articles like intoxicating beverages, and, possibly, tobacco; finally, some more elastic taxes which could readily be raised or lowered according to the needs of the federal treasury. Among our "ideal" taxes, one, perhaps, on the gross revenues of railroads engaged in inter-state commerce could be recommended.

The disadvantage of relying entirely on customs duties has been amply demonstrated by American experience. When largest revenues are needed, they yield least; when least is needed, they yield most. We have suffered embarrassment and the loss of countless millions by the failure in the past to maintain a satisfactory scheme of internal revenue taxation, and it is to be hoped that this mistake will not be repeated.

I trust that this brief and inadequate sketch of my ideas in regard to a few federal problems may prove suggestive which is the most I hope for. RICHARD T. ELY.

SHALL THE INTERNAL REVENUE BE RETAINED?

By Professor Richmond M. Smith, of Columbia College.

The existence of the present surplus and its probable continuance bring up two questions demanding solution in the present session of Congress. The first is, what shall be done to get rid of the accumulation of money in the federal treasury, and the money which will accumulate before any laws looking to the final reduction of revenue can take effect; and the second is in what way revenue can be permanently reduced so as to correspond with the demands of government. The first is a temporary difficulty and can be met by temporary measures. The second is much the more serious question, for it threatens to involve the whole future financial policy of the United States. I shall, therefore, consider it first, and devote only a few words at the close to the former. I shall also take it for granted that there should be no consideration paid to schemes for balancing accounts by extravagant expenditures made for the purpose of getting rid of the surplus, or to the absurd proposal to raise protective duties to a point where they would be prohibitive and there would be no income. The permanent reduction of taxation is the only way of bringing the expenditures and the receipts of the government into equilibrium. This brings us at once to the question whether this reduction shall take place in the internal revenue or in the customs duties. This question can best be approached by posing the further question : Do we want to abandon the present system of internal revenue on whisky, beer, and tobacco? They are articles which are taxed the world over as high as it is possible to tax them. They are recognized the world over as luxuries which people are perfectly able to do without. They are consumed in immense quantities, so that the revenue from them is always large. At the same time they possess in a remarkable degree the quality of elasticity, that is, when people are poor they can easily diminish their consumption of them, while in good times they can increase the quantity or the quality consumed. The burden of taxation thus naturally and automatically adjusts itself to the condition of the community. The burden decreases when people are less able to pay, while the revenue steadily increases with the prosperity of the country and its growth in wealth and population. The use of these articles is only slowly affected by changes in taste and fashion, and thus there is no danger of the revenue disappearing. In the universality of their consumption they resemble articles of necessity, while in the possibility of the individual doing without them they are luxuries. Other articles which resemble them in the first respect, like sugar, coffee, tea, and salt, are recognized as necessaries of life among all civilized nations, while other luxuries, like wine, laces, velvet, etc., are not largely enough consumed to give a great revenue and are subject to changes of taste and fashion.

It would seem to me a serious financial mistake for the federal government to give up such a source of revenue, which is large in itself, and which will always be a sure means of income. It is not well for the government to rely exclusively on customs for its taxes. They depend for their imposition too much on other considerations, such as those of a protective system, and for their yield on the condition of commerce and the prosperity of trade. Many of them impose a much greater burden upon the people than they return to the treasury. Many of them are most unequal in the way they rest on particular industries or particular classes. At any rate it is utterly impossible in many cases to determine what the exact burden is and where it really rests. In the greater portion of our present tariff we are absolutely "going it blind" as far as the financial consequences of the impositions are concerned. No human mind can trace out the real effect of these customs duties on the industry and the social development of the people of the United States. This is said neither from the standpoint of a free-trader, nor of a protectionist, nor of a socialist. The present tariff is so complex that no one can tell how far it really aids the industries of the country and how far it cripples them. No one can tell how far it keeps up the wages of workingmen and how far it throws the burden of taxation on them. Is it not sufficient to raise two-thirds of the national revenue by these taxes, the burden of which and the incidence of which are so uncertain? Is it sound finance to abandon an income of $100,000,000 raised by a simple and easy tax on luxuries, the burden and incidence of which we *do* know, and raise it by taxes, the financial effects of which we do *not* know? To abandon the internal revenue system means that the present revenue from customs will be insufficient or barely sufficient to meet the wants of the government in time of peace. That means that any revision of the present tariff will be practically impossible for a long time to come, for no revision of the tariff is possible except in the presence of a surplus revenue or the means of providing a revenue in case of a deficit. When the English revised their tariff it was with the help of the income tax. Our means of tiding over any deficiency following changes in the tariff is the internal revenue; and once destroy the organization and it will never be possible to restore it except in some great crisis like a war. But he would be a bold man who would affirm that the present tariff is perfect even from the standpoint of protection to home industries. He would be a still bolder man who would affirm that the present tariff is just in its burden on the poor man. And no man would be found bold enough to affirm that the present tariff has any claim to consideration as a financial measure. But why abandon the possibility of revision either from the standpoint of a sound policy of encouragement to home industry, or of a sound social policy of the exemption of the poor from undue burdens, or of a sound financial policy of making the taxes as productive and as little burdensome as possible? There is no danger of the overthrow of the doctrine of protection in this country. The democracy is too powerful and finds representation in the legislative body too easily not to be sure to have all its wishes complied with the moment they are expressed. Democracy, too, always demands an immediate remedy for any evil it may be suffering under. Our tendency is and always will be to apply protection to any industry the moment it seems to be languishing. That has been the experience of France since the establishment of the republic. But what we want and what democracy will want in the long run is protection wisely applied. We do not want protection for everybody and for everything, for that means a burden on everybody and on everything. We do not want protection always because there has been protection once, for that means that we are to pay no attention to changes in industry and methods of production. In other words, even from the protectionist standpoint, the tariff must be subject to more or less constant revision. It is not necessary to show that from the standpoint of social burdens and of financial policy we should also retain in our hands the power of revising our customs duties when necessary.

It would also, in my opinion, be a serious political blunder for the federal government to abandon the internal revenue system. No one can tell what the future financial demands of the government are to be. It is always well to have two strings to your bow. In case of failure of the revenue from duties owing to a depression of trade or interruption to commerce, the internal revenue must make good the deficiency. In case of some financial emergency, like a war, the internal revenue system is already established, the people are accustomed to it, and it is easy to increase the revenue by increasing the rate of taxation. In case it is abandoned the whole system will have to be re-established, and this will be a matter of time and probably of more or less friction and opposition. Some of the states will doubtless have appropriated the taxes, and they will have to be ousted, and the United States resume the position which it ought never to have given up. It is said that the internal revenue collector is hateful, and that the man who represents simply the fiscal power of a distant government ought to be removed. I believe that is one reason why he should be retained. The government of the United States is the government of the whole people, and there is no reason why its officers should not be everywhere. The internal revenue collector is no more hateful than the custom house official, and if the frontier is to have the one why should not the interior have the other? The Secretary of the Treasury has said that the two services could be combined so that the expense would be no greater than is necessary for an efficient customs administration. It would be foolish to abandon these articles to be excised by the different states, for then we should have different rates of taxation, different administrative systems, and infinitely more expense.

Some persons advocate retaining the internal revenue tax on whiskey but giving it up at least on tobacco. It is said that tobacco, if not a necessary of life, is one of the comforts, and to the men who use it it has become practically a necessity. The tax on domestic tobacco rests on the poor and the men of moderate means, for the rich use imported tobacco. To give up the tax on tobacco would relieve the surplus to the extent of thirty millions, which would leave plenty of margin to reduce the customs.

I do not sympathize with this movement to take off the tax on tobacco. It is an attack on the internal revenue system, and when the tobacco tax is gone it will be easy to remove the excise on beer, and then on whiskey. I do not believe that tobacco is a necessary of life in the sense that sugar, tea, coffee and blankets are necessaries of life. I think that if we are going to help the poor man we had better give him free sugar, salt, iron tools, and woollen clothing for himself and his children. Would not the states immediately tax the tobacco if it were freed from federal taxation, so that the poor man would still miss his cheap pipe? The tax is not a heavy one. By far the larger portion is paid on manufactured tobacco, at the rate of eight cents per pound, and on cigars at the rate of three dollars per thousand. It is not a very severe burden upon the laboring man to pay to the government one-half cent for each ounce of tobacco that he smokes, and for the man of moderate means to pay one-third of a cent for each cigar. The number of adult males in the United States is probably about fifteen millions, which would make a tax of less than two dollars a head.

We must also remember that this is a tax which the laboring man pays as a rule only on his own consumption, while the tax on sugar or on blankets and woollens he pays on the consumption of his whole family. If the tax is too heavy, reduce the rate. Sweep away the petty license taxes on the manufacturers, dealers and peddlers, and make the tax simple and so that the price of the article will be increased only by the amount of the tax. I do not believe that any of the internal revenue taxes should be used for sumptuary purposes. That should be left to the states to regulate by the imposition of licenses or by prohibitory laws.

If, now, the internal revenue is to be retained, the reduction must occur in the customs duties. It has been indicated above where this reduction ought to take place. The sugar duties ought to be entirely removed; then the duties on raw wool, and gradually those on woollen goods. Then ought to come the duties on salt, lumber, and other raw materials. At the same time we ought to put on the free list all articles the duties on which are not protective, and the removal of which would not affect appreciably the protective system. The sugar duties alone would relieve us of fifty millions, and should be entirely removed; for a simple reduction in the rate would not necessarily reduce the revenue in the same proportion.

In regard to the question of what shall be done to get rid of the surplus which has already accumulated, and which will accumulate before the new tax laws can go into effect, I see no objection to the plan of Mr. John Jay Knox to anticipate the payment of a portion of the interest on the bonds, and to substitute two and one-half per cent bonds for the present four and four and a half per cents.

RICHMOND M. SMITH.

A DEFENSE OF THE PROTECTIVE POLICY.

By Professor Robert Ellis Thompson, of the University of Pennsylvania.

My views on the duty of Congress in the matter of national taxation and revenue are based upon a study of the fiscal history of our government, carried on for more than fifteen years in the discharge of the duties of my professorship.

In 1787-89 the states surrendered to the nation the right to impose duties on imports and exports. They did so in compliance with the necessities of the country at that time. They did not suppose that they also were giving up the other great form of indirect taxation — excises upon the manufacture and consumption of certain commodities. They have found by experience that this also was given up at that time, and that nobody but the national government can levy such taxes, except in the form of licenses to carry on certain kinds of business. As these licenses bring in but a small revenue, the states and the local governments inside the states have to provide for their needs by direct taxes on houses, land, incomes, and personal property. The consequence is that their revenues are hard to collect and the influence of the tax-payer keeps the tax-rate down to the lowest figure possible.

In 1787-89 there was also a transfer of certain duties and their expenses from the states to the nation. But the spirit of colonial jealousy, which still prevailed at the formation of our government, made the transfer as small as possible. When we compare the American with any other system of government, we find our national government has less to do, and the local governments it includes, has more, than under any other fiscal system. The states gave up all the easy and ample sources of revenue, and yet retained nearly all the expensive functions of administration. From this, two bad consequences have followed :

1. The work left to the states has been done very badly. The tax-rate has been low in most of them, and kept low to attract capital and industry. In a few, as for instance Massachusetts, it has been very high, and industries not specially favored by local circumstances have been driven from the state. In Boston, nearly everything you see bears the mark of some town in the Middle States as the place where it was produced. In the average American state the roads are disgraceful to our civilization, the schools starved, illiteracy on the increase. And many have been tempted by poverty to the partial or complete repudiation of their debts.

2. A surplus of national revenue has been a constantly recurring fact in our fiscal history. Hamilton forestalled its early appearance by the assumption of the debts of the states, soon after the government was set going. Jefferson notified Congress of its approach in 1806, protested against any reduction of the tariff to get rid of it, and proposed rather to amend the Constitution so as to transfer more duties and expenses to the national government. The war of 1812 postponed the appearance of a surplus until Jackson's time. But he foresaw it, and in his first message to Congress, in 1829, he advised that the surplus be distributed among the states. This was actually done in 1836, but the tariff of 1835, and its consequence, the panic of 1837, removed the need of it by reducing the revenues of the government below its expenses. But distribution had worked so well that the Whigs, in 1842, tried to make it a permanent feature of our policy, and were prevented by the veto of President Tyler. The Democrats came back to power, and their tariff legislation and fiscal mismanagement staved off a surplus so well, that when the war for the Union broke out the country owed a considerable debt, and was paying 6 and 7 per cent interest on much of it. The war, and the debt thus incurred, absorbed all the national revenue until last year, and will again absorb it after 1891.

The present situation is not exactly that of 1836. Then the national payment of debt had come to an end. Now we face an interval of only three years in which it must be suspended. Shall we destroy the debt paying power of the national government during those three years, with the certainty of finding great difficulty in restoring it ? All proposals for a wholesale reduction of revenue are proposals to destroy it.

It therefore seems best to me to reduce no revenue but that from the tax on alcohol used in the arts, and the duty on unrefined sugar, and the latter only after it has been ascertained that we cannot make sugar from sorghum enough to meet our needs. That delay we owe, not to the sugar planters, but to the Western farmer. I think whiskey and tobacco both are good things to tax. My experience as an educator convinces me that tobacco is doing nearly as much harm to the rising generation as is alcohol to persons of mature years.

Mr. Cleveland has proposed to reduce the revenue by reduction of the rates of duty imposed by the tariff. To this there are several weighty objections :

1. It would be quite impossible to effect any such reduction without putting duties down to a free trade level, and robbing the tariff entirely of its productive character. Very high duties might be reduced to a strictly protective level,

with the result of reducing the revenue. But since the revision of 1883, there are few if any such duties in the tariff. Any further reduction would tend to greatly increase imports, and would thus increase the revenue, unless the duties are made very low or the free lists greatly increased. The bill proposed by Mr. Mills would remit some $22,000,000, by transfers, mostly objectionable, to the free list. But almost the whole of this reduction would be swallowed up in the increase of revenue which this reduction on other articles would cause, by increasing importations. Indeed, the most effective way to reduce the revenue from the tariff, would be to raise the duties on those articles which we can produce at home, but do not, for want of proper protection. Such are tin-plates, worsted and woollen goods, the finer cotton fabrics, iron for structural purposes, and many others. A high duty on these would produce less revenue by diminishing imports.

(2) There is nothing in the relation of the present tariff to the needs of producers or of consumers, or to the industrial situation generally, which calls for any general reduction of its duties. The *producers* are favored by it to such an extent that our national wealth is growing more rapidly than ever before. In the long period, from 1607 to 1850, the total of accumulation was only fourteen billions of dollars. In the

two decades, 1860-1880, we added to this thirty billions, making a total of forty-four billions in 1880. We already exceed England in the aggregate of wealth, and by 1890 it probably will be found that the average share of wealth will be greater in America. At the same the more even *distribution* of wealth has gone forward. Imagination fastens itself upon the great fortunes of the few. In no other wealthy country, however, is so small a part of the aggregate gathered into what are called "fortunes." The $780,000,000 in American savings banks is only a fraction of the total accumulation of the working classes. In our own city very little is hoarded in that way, most of the savings of the wage-earners being invested in real estate through our building associations. Neither can it be said with truth that *consumers* are oppressed by the tariff. There is not an article of necessity or comfort, whose importation is restricted by the tariff, which is not greatly cheapened since I first saw America in 1857, when the country was enjoying the "blessings" of free trade. Mr. Edward Atkinson reports a fall of from 26 to 46 per cent. along the whole line of necessary articles since 1861, while the yearly wages of a skilled mechanic have risen from $468 to $720; and Mr. Atkinson is a free trader. By enlarging the basis of supply we have put an end to foreign monopolies of our market. By diverting the dormant capital and energies of the nation into manufacturing industries, we have established a home competition which has brought prices to a normal level. Even the consumer who produces nothing and has nothing to sell will find that his money goes farther than it did thirty years ago. But the average American is a consumer who also produces, and who, therefore, is interested not only in the price of what he has to buy, but also in the price of what he has to sell. Practically, he buys by exchanging his commodity for others which he needs. And this sort of trade is always most favorable when he can effect such an exchange with his own neighbors and thus save the cost of transportation. Especially the producer of food and of raw materials finds the relation of prices most in his favor when he is located near to the place where these are converted into manufactured articles. The object of protection is to bring the artisan and the manufacturer into neighborhood with the farmer. The stimulus given to the growth of agriculture by the homestead law has prevented this being attained as yet. But we are coming fast toward it. Free trade would check the process.

(3.) The great immigration to the United States, especially from free trade countries like Ireland and Norway, shows that protection has helped to make America more attractive. The cheapness of everything in money, which is the free trade idol, prevails in these countries to the utmost. Their people fly from this cheapness to a land where the *relation of prices* is favorable to the producing classes. An Irishman was heard complaining that he could buy as much for a shilling at home as for a dollar in America. "Why didn't you stay there?" he was asked. "Bedad, I couldn't get the shillin'," was his candid answer. His labor, the one commodity he had to sell, would not bring him even the shilling in a country whose industries have been desolated, all but annihilated, by English competition. But he could get the dollar in a country which takes care of its industrial interests. That is why 8,620,664 people sought a new home in America during the years 1861–1886, mostly from free trade countries. And yet many of them are seeking to overthrow by their votes the very policy which has made America desirable to them.

ROBERT ELLIS THOMPSON.

THE READJUSTMENT OF THE REVENUES.

By Professor Edwin R. A. Seligman, of Columbia College.

The one great danger which menaces the financial equilibrium and thus the commercial prosperity of the country, is the existence of the surplus. No words are too strong to set forth its demoralizing effects, or the vicious and unscientific doctrines of which it is the result. In any discussion of the situation from the standpoint of the science of finance, the necessity of curtailing the surplus must be taken for granted. Only on this assumption can any intelligent propositions be advanced.

The question thus before the country is primarily a question of taxation. The necessity of cutting off some of the objects of taxation being granted, the problem is to ascertain from a broad standpoint what are the most fitting sources of national revenue. It would be easy to show that our American system of taxation is wofully out of date. There is no civilized country in the world with a greater actual (though not ostensible) inequality in its general tax system—an inequality which is not universally perceived simply because of the small proportion which our direct taxes bear to the income of the people. In a well digested system the national taxation should be so arranged as to correct in some measure the apparent inequalities of our state and local taxation. But it would be going too far out of the way in this place to show in what these inequalities of local taxation consist, and in what lines a reform should take place. We must confine ourselves to the national system and to suggestions for its improvement.

Let us grant that indirect taxes are most suitable for the general government. Ought we now to curtail the import duties or the internal revenue? The answer is unfortunately not one that can be given solely by the science of finance. From the standpoint of finance the customs tariff would be simply a tariff for revenue, and its provisions could be so arranged as to produce the greatest revenue with the smallest burdens. But ever since the beginning of our government the revenue feature of the tariff has been inextricably intertwined with the industrial or protective feature. It has been and will be for many years impossible to divorce these two considerations. And it is doubtful whether they ought to be entirely divorced. The doctrine of free trade, even in the sense of tariff for revenue only, can no longer claim absolute and unswerving allegiance from the advocates of historical economics. The sway of the Manchester school is gone, never to return. Sound economic doctrine does indeed regard the freest trade as the goal, the aim; it looks upon protection as permissible only so far as it may eventually lead to free trade. A protection which does not protect, and which will not in a fairly measureable period render itself unnecessary, is a fraud and a delusion. Just as the only justification of state interference in general is the education of the citizens to liberty, so the only national plea for protection is the expectation that it will make free trade possible. That this expectation has frequently failed of realization is clear to any student of our tariff history. But it is not permissible to claim with the orthodox free traders that this expectation can never in any particular case be realized.

While it may therefore be freely confessed that many of the protectionist's arguments are unsound, and that our present tariff may fairly lay claim in some respects to the classic term "tariff of abominations," it would be highly injudicious to demand a sweeping reform in the sense of tariff for revenue alone. We can not make *tabula rasa* of all our protective duties. The most feasible plan seems to be to abolish or diminish the duties on raw materials as far as possible, and on those commodities in which experience and study have disclosed an incapacity to be protected or "nurtured" into vigorous life. To protect simply for the sake of maintaining an otherwise unsuitable industry is, with rare exceptions, to impose a burden on the public without obtaining any compensating advantages in the end.

A horizontal reduction of import duties, such as is meant by "tariff for revenue" alone, and which would imply in our present situation a complete retention or perhaps even an increase of the internal revenue taxes, seems therefore not to recommend itself. But does it follow, on the other hand, as is frequently claimed, that the whole internal revenue system should be abolished and entire reliance be placed on customs duties? To this proposition the science of finance can give a categorical answer.

Indirect taxes were in their origin indeed imposts or impositions, rather than taxes. The excises were at first entirely arbitrary, and sinned against the fundamental principles of equality and universality of taxation. Even at the formation of the present government, the popular feeling against excises was exceedingly strong. They were declared by many unworthy of free citizens. But at present we must regard the matter from a wider point of view. Reliance on any one single form of taxation has become an impossibility in our highly complex civilization. The inequality and inquisitorial character of our excises are to-day certainly no greater than in the case of our chief direct taxes. But, above all, attention must be given to this one controlling consideration. A fundamental demand of a sound system is elasticity of revenue. Such elasticity can be obtained only by a general income or property tax, or by a well considered excise system. But revenue from customs duties is essentially inelastic. As a general income or property tax seems out of the question for the national government (although from the standpoint of pure finance its expediency might at least be discussed) it follows that a retention of the internal revenue is necessary, even if only in part. To completely abandon all the internal taxes, with the entire machinery of assessment and collection, would be a great mistake. To-day we have a surplus; in a few years, whether owing to some particular exigency or not, we may have a deficit. To again call into being the whole system of internal taxes, as we did in the war of 1812 and during the rebellion, would be as it was then, a slow and laborious undertaking. But with the machinery and the system already existing, it would be easy to engraft on the existing plan the new additions which might become necessary.

Looked at from the broadest possible standpoint, the best and most elastic system would be a form of income tax. I know of the widespread opposition to this tax in the United States. But if its history will ever be impartially written, it will be seen that the outcry was in a great measure a groundless one. A carefully devised general income tax like that in Great Britain or on the continent could attain two results. It could as a supplementary tax most surely correct the inequalities of our State and local systems, and it would be far more elastic than any other system. We would not then be chronically troubled with the danger of surplus and of deficit financiering. But in our actual situation, where there is no proposition from any side for a national income tax, and where the chief question is the abolition or retention of our internal taxes, the answer given by the science of finance is sufficiently plain: Retain in part at least the internal revenue.

The proposition to abolish both the whiskey and the tobacco taxes may hence be brushed aside as unworthy of acceptance. As to the choice between the tobacco tax and customs duties, it is perhaps difficult to give a definite answer. Certain portions of the tariff should at all events be immediately abrogated. Taxes on raw materials like that on wool have at present no adequate justification. What the wool grower gains the woollen manufacturer loses, and the public at large certainly derive no compensating advantages from the increased price. The same is true of many other raw materials. No consideration except the vague sense of property in vested interests can rightfully demand the further retention of these taxes. The hollowness of the pauper labor argument need, of course, not be exposed to students of political economy. But the absurdity of a system which attempts with one hand to bolster up our manufacturing industries, and with the other to handicap them by increasing the prime cost, must become painfully apparent to all logical minds. The first condition of successful competition with foreign products is liberation of the raw materials.

To discuss the separate points further than this would be difficult in the present short paper. It would be necessary to call attention to many other considerations, such as regard for the interests of the poor, choice of those commodities whose supply is least fluctuating, and the selection of luxuries as pre-eminently fit objects of taxation. But a tariff arranged on truly scientific principles can be attained only when based on financial and not on protective considerations. The complexity of the problem arises chiefly from the fact that a compromise is necessary between the tariff for revenue and the tariff for protection.   EDWIN R. A. SELIGMAN.

THE THEORY AND PRACTICE OF PROTECTION.

By Professor Jesse Macy, of Iowa College.

The system which will in the end best conduce to the protection and upbuilding of American industries is to be found through a low rate of taxation. The United States has enjoyed an advantage over competing nations of the old world because, notwithstanding the cost of the civil war and the extinction of a large portion of the national debt, the rate of taxation has been comparatively low. When the civil war was ended the armies of the two sections were added at once to the productive energies of the country. Had we kept these armies in the field, and had we called into existence a navy of corresponding dimensions, our national debt could not so easily have been paid, and all the productive industries of the country would have been crippled by excessive taxation. With the final disappearance of the national debt and a corresponding relief from the burdens of taxation American industries will be still more favored. Every extravagant or unnecessary expenditure is an injury to the prosperity of the people. No form of taxation can be other than a burden, and as such it cripples the industries of the country.

The people of the United States believe most thoroughly in a policy of encouragement to home industries. Often the citizens of a town pay large sums of money to establish in their midst a new wealth-producing industry. Or, they exempt for a term of years from the burdens of local taxation new manufactories. This may often be a wise policy. An injury for the time is incurred by the older industries, but in the end a helpful burden-sharer is secured. As with a town or neighborhood, so with the nation at large; certain great industries may be introduced and permanently established by burdening for a term of years the industries already established. This may be done through a protective tariff. Such a tariff is for the time being a burden and an injury to the older industries already established, but in the end this injury may be more than repaired by the advantages arising from the new industry.

To apply to our existing system of taxation the teachings of political economy, it is necessary to understand clearly certain particulars in this teaching. Not every doctrine which has borne the name of protection has received support from recognized economists. Henry C. Carey has perhaps done more than any other writer to commend to Americans a doctrine of protection, and he taught most explicitly that a protective tariff could not properly be relied upon for the revenues of the government. It is, he maintained, a temporary expedient to attain a definite object, and when that object is attained the tax should cease. The object of protection, as defined by Carey, was first to diversify American industries and then to establish free trade with all the world. The statesmen and economists who first taught a doctrine of protection did not teach that a permanent burden should be laid upon the many industries for the benefit of a few. They taught also that one object of protection was to make commodities cheaper. They admitted that for a time the particular commodity favored by the protective tariff would be made dearer, and that those buying the dear commodity are thus injured. But, when the new industry has been secured, the commodity would be cheaper than it would otherwise be, and thus the injury would be repaired. The original protectionists were not opposed to a policy of free trade. Carey complained that the so-called free traders had filched the name which more properly belonged to his school. He looked forward to the time when free trade should be established upon an enduring basis. The free trader maintained that all should have the right to buy in the cheapest and sell in the dearest market. Protectionists admitted that this is true, but claimed that a community or a nation should also have the right to buy anything they pleased, included a new wealth-producing industry. The doctrine of protection as thus stated is not in conflict with the doctrine of free trade, but is a rather more comprehensive statement of the doctrine.

John Stuart Mill is not ordinarily classified as a protectionist, yet in one famous paragraph he entirely justifies on scientific grounds the theory that, in a new country, for the attainment of a new industry, a temporary protective tariff may be imposed. Professor Sidgewick, of Cambridge, England, in a more recent work on Political Economy, maintains that on pure theoretical grounds the protectionists have an advantage over so-called free traders; that a theory of protection may be maintained. The difficulty with protection is not so much in the theory as in the practice. It is difficult to forsee just what industries may be introduced and in a reasonable time become self supporting. Mistakes may be made in the selection of the industries to be favored by a protective tariff. By mistakes in this regard a nation may have fastened upon the people a group of exotic industries which tend to permanently injure all others. Professor Sidgewick says that because of the practical difficulties which arise in working out a policy of protection it may in the end be wiser for statesmen to adhere to the narrower and less scientific theory of free trade. The strict free trade theory would require that a duty should be collected only on commodities not produced in the country; or, if a tax is collected on an import which is produced in the country, an excise equal to the duty should also be collected from the domestic product. Thus a duty upon spices or coffee is not inconsistent with the free trade theory. Nor is a duty on tobacco, if the duty is not more than the excise on tobacco.

If we examine our actual tariff list we find that it is not consistent with any theory of taxation that has ever been taught. Some items in the list are not inconsistent with the theory of free trade. Other items were, at least originally, justified by the doctrine of protection as set forth by standard authorities, while some of the items are not and never were justified by any rational theory of taxation. As an illustration of the latter class, I would mention the duty on timber and lumber. The changing of wooded lands into barren wastes is not a wealth-producing industry. The government has expended large sums of money to preserve forests, while at the same time it has maintained a tax which has led directly to a wasteful destruction of most valuable forests. Such a tax is not a protective tariff, it is a destructive tariff. Besides the destruction of wealth which has been caused by the duty on timber, every wealth-producing industry in the country has been permanently injured. Timber and lumber have been made dear, and for the injury thus inflicted there is no compensation.

The duty upon wool is a tax not justified by a rational doctrine of protection. The majority of farmers are consumers and not producers of wool. It is not fair that these should be burdened for the benefit of the few. Common woollen goods should be furnished to the masses of the people as cheaply as they can be made. Our woollen manufactories should be permitted freely to purchase their materials in all parts of the world. They will then be able to compete with others in the sale of common woollen goods. A permanent duty may properly be laid upon some of the finer grades of cloth. This may be justified on the ground of luxury. The burden will fall chiefly upon those best able to bear it, and our own manufacturers will be slightly favored and encouraged in the production of clothes of the highest grades. A similar policy should hold in dealing with iron and all other materials. The burden should be removed first from the crude forms and those most widely used. This will serve as a direct stimulus to the great industries not favored by a monopoly tariff.

In dealing with our actual list it may be found as a matter of experience that we have some costly and independent industries called into existence by a mistaken tariff. It would not be just or right now to deal with our tariff quite as if these industries did not exist. It may be wise to continue to support some of them for a good many years, rather than pursue an alternative policy. Yet such industries should hold a language and decorum properly befitting their condition. The revision of our tariff should proceed with a firm and steady hand until by actual experiment the really "pauper" industries are discovered. It will be impossible to state in advance who are paupers and who are not. Many may think themselves paupers who would find through the relief from present burdens a prosperity never before realized. J. Macy.

THE CERTAINTIES OF THE TARIFF QUESTION.

By Professor John B. Clark, of Smith College.

A hundred years of discussion concerning protective tariffs have not gone for nothing. Some things are settled. They may be disputed by the unintelligent; but men of discernment who have given attention to the subject are agreed concerning them. These points of agreement do not decide the entire question; it is possible to admit them and to continue a protectionist, a free trader, or a conservative revenue reformer. It is possible for a man belonging to either of these three classes to give a reason for his faith; but it must be a different reason from that which would have served the purpose twenty-five years ago. A discussion of the tariff may with advantage begin by a statement of these incontrovertible points.

1. A protective duty cannot raise wages in the protected industry as compared with the standard prevailing in other occupations. Spinners of silk do not get more per day than spinners of cotton, by reason of the high duty on silk thread; nor would they do so if the duty on silk were quadrupled. If a tariff raises wages at all it must accomplish it by increasing

the general reward of labor. It must raise wages in agriculture, in transportation, and in commerce, as well as in manufactures.

2. Real wages are to be estimated, not in money, but in commodities. To give a workman ten per cent. more in money than he formerly received, and to raise by fifteen per cent the prices of the articles he must buy, would be to lower his wages. It follows from these two principles that no tariff can raise the wages of any workman except by increasing the real reward of all workmen. If it is to benefit a shoe laster or an iron molder it must at the same time give to the plowman on the Dakota farm and to the cow-boy on the Montana ranch more commodities for a day's labor.

3. Wages are gauged in amount by the productiveness of industry. When land can be had for the asking, wages are what a man can get by cultivating it; and if the land is both fertile and accessible, wages are high. Manufacturers must pay enough to induce their men to keep out of agricultural life. They can afford to pay this amount if their business creates as large a product as could be created by the same expenditure of labor and capital upon the soil. If the product of the business is smaller it cannot survive. Natural selection insures, in a new country, the survival of the most productive industries.

4. High wages, **caused by the great productiveness of labor applied to land**, are the primary fact in the history of American industry. Before the war of 1812, and the imposition of the tariff of 1816, only those industries could subsist that could afford to pay the high wages obtainable in agriculture. These were the industries that created the largest real product. Protection diverts labor to less productive occupations.

(5) A tariff that "protects" anything does so by taxing the more productive industries in order to sustain the less productive. A protective duty on woolen goods does not enable a day's labor in a mill to create a particle more of cloth than it would have created before; but it causes a day's labor on the farm to purchase a smaller amount of cloth than it would otherwise have done. A tariff on manufactured articles lessens the economic product of agriculture; it gives a bushel of wheat a smaller purchasing power. It leaves to the farmer a smaller wage-paying power. As agricultural wages set the standard to which the returns of all labor conform, the protective duties lower that general standard. Labor in the mill must henceforth be paid at the rate that now prevails on the farm. That, however, is a reduced rate; protection has lessened the reward of labor even in the **protected industry**.

(6) It follows that protection necessarily inflicts an economic loss on the country that resorts to it, by diverting labor and capital from industries that create a large real product to those that create a smaller one. It lessens general wages by lowering the standard to which they must conform. It makes the country poorer, and inflicts the loss largely on the poorer class within the country.

Do these points, if conceded, decide the tariff question as now presented in the United States? Not at all. We have to deal with an existing tariff, and we know perfectly well that we shall not, in fact, so deal with it as to crush an existing industry. A business that needs protection will continue to have it, whatever may be the effects upon the country at large. Moreover, it is not certain that the loss entailed by protection will prove permanent. The "infant industry" argument has some basis in fact and reason; and recent experience enables us to so supplement it as to add to the certainties of the tariff question a point that somewhat favors the protective side, and that serves to reconcile us to the impossibility of any radical changes in our present system.

Only unproductive industries need protection; and this unproductiveness may diminish with time. The processes may be learned, a market for the goods may be secured, and new machinery may be invented. The infant may actually grow. But the question that decides the capacity of an industry to survive is its relative, not its absolute, productiveness. It needs only to be as productive as agriculture in order to be able to pay equally high wages and to stand unprotected on its feet. What if agriculture itself becomes less productive with time? Is it not clear that industries that formerly could not subsist may then do so?

The history of the United States presents two striking facts; and to place them in juxtaposition is all that I need farther to attempt. Infant agriculture has been abnormally productive. It has not been land culture, in any true sense, but land spoliation. It has been a wresting from the soil of its original endowment of fertility. It has been an exporting of the better elements of our soil in the ships that have carried wheat and flour to Liverpool. Infant manufactures have been abnormally unproductive. They have incurred the initial losses incident to experimentation, to imperfect work and lack of established markets. Time makes them more productive. Time makes agriculture less productive, and lessens the standard of profitableness that an industry must attain in order to subsist without protection. Many particular duties are tending to become unnecessary; the industries that they protect are advancing toward a point where they can subsist without them. When that point is reached the American manufacturer can supply the home demand, and without farther lowering his price can hold his market against the foreign competitor. The duty that has protected him will become inoperative.

It is among the certainties of the subject that duties on raw materials tend to prevent manufactures from attaining the point of independence. They are wholly irrational. Their origin is political, not economic. They grow out of the scramble that takes place in the lobbies of Congress for sops for many constituencies. A vote-catching policy on the part of men and parties may save some of them for a time; in reason they are already condemned, and by the test of farther experience they are destined to be more emphatically condemned.

JOHN B. CLARK.

TAXATION AND APPROPRIATION.

By Professor Woodrow Wilson, of Bryn Mawr College.

Probably a very considerable majority of the thinking people of the country are of the opinion that some sort of revision of our present tariff laws ought to be undertaken. Those laws were passed under very exceptional circumstances; they are full of complexities and absurdities of the most irritating and unnecessary sort; and they yield a revenue greatly in excess of the needs of the government, as well as at some points altogether unnecessary for purposes of protection. So ripe are they for alteration, indeed, that probably the more far-sighted even among those who are most benefited by them would prefer to endure considerable reductions of their present advantages—if only the changes made gave promise of permanency of policy—rather than continue to undergo the constant alarms of legislative tinkering with which a perpetuation of the anomalies and extravagances of the existing system is sure to vex them. The question is, What sort of a revision; on what lines and for what purposes?

No discussion of the interior defects of our present tariff laws would be adequate which did

not go into their details; and probably very few besides treasury experts could handle those details with any confidence. For those who look at the tariff from the outside, in its general features and in its bearings upon the general questions of federal finance, interest centres in the three facts of a protective policy, an enormous surplus, and a choice between license taxes on whiskey and tobacco and import duties as sources of revenue. At heart the tariff question is a question of taxation, and such a question of taxation as carries with it some of the most momentous questions of government. The existence of a revenue greatly in excess of the needs of the government is generally looked at almost exclusively in the light of its influence on Congress; a more suggestive view of it may be had if it be considered in its effects upon the political habits of the people at large. Of course, with unlimited sums of money awaiting its vote, Congress will be constantly under an almost irresistible temptation to spendthrift habits of appropriation. It may be expected to look about diligently for thorough means of spending the immense income at its disposal. It is even under a sort of financial constraint to spend. Not to spend is to allow money to be piled up in the treasury; and no extravagance can be worse in its financial results than that. The whole case is bad enough;

but apparently betterment is past praying for so long as the surplus exists.

Look now at the other side of the picture, the relations of the people to their government. Money is being spent without new taxation; and appropriation without *accompanying* taxation is as bad as taxation without representation. The people do not feel, any more than Congress feels, that the money expended so lavishly *is being* extracted from the pockets of commerce and the professions. It was, so to say, extracted a long time ago, when the tariff laws were enacted. The policy of protection is neither here nor there, when the matter is looked at from this point of view. That policy was fixed upon long ago; so far as present legislation is concerned taxation is based upon no policy at all—there is no taxation. Congress and the people are accepting a fact; they are not choosing a course of action.

In order to the preservation of political health under a popular constitution, taxation and appropriation must go hand in hand. There is as much need, and the same need, that taxation should be annually renewed, annually re-originated, as that appropriations should be annually renewed and re-originated. If protection be considered a legitimate object of taxation, it may annually be declared so, just as taxation to meet the running expenses of the government is;

and it ought, if sound political views are to prevail, to be thus annually voted an object of taxation. The destination of the revenue so raised ought also to be every year determined; the revenue, over and above government expenses, ought to be applied to some particular object every year, to the last dollar that it is safe to promise in advance of the verification of calculations. Nobody claims that protection is equally desirable and beneficial at all times for all countries, as the payment of debts and their interest is. The conditions of the trade and industry of a country change from decade to decade, and even from year to year, and tariffs ought to be sensitive to such changes. If the tariff be the embodiment of a just policy, as it is, untouched and inflexible from year to year, how much more just might it be made by careful modifications periodically undertaken!

At any rate, *the people ought to be made to feel their fiscal policy all the time;* otherwise they will never give regular or adequate head to it. And there would seem to be no room for doubt that the country *feels* the whiskey and tobacco license tax much more than it feels the duties on imports. It shows consciousness of the one, habitual unconsciousness of the other. These license taxes, then, are the best indirect taxes that can be laid, for a double reason: they are taxes which the people—or at any rate a very talkative and imperative part of the people—feel that they are paying; and they fall upon articles of luxury, not upon articles of necessity.

An ideal financial policy is easy enough to describe and wish for; it has hitherto in the world's experience proved a very difficult thing to attain to. Such a policy would have, to suit the United States at present, one special feature: it would not hasten the payment of the national debt, because haste in that direction under existing circumstances would involve more inconveniences, both financial and political, than advantages of any sort. Such a policy—an ideal financial policy—would include for every state the joining hand to hand of appropriation and taxation; would make them inseparable parts of one and the same policy. Whatever may be taken as the ground and measure of taxation—whether the expenses of the government plus protection, or the expenses of the government only—that ought also to be made the ground and measure of appropriation. No nation, if it is to retain the acute sense of responsibility which ought always to accompany the exercise of the financial functions of the body politic, ought ever to have a policy of taxation without having a policy of appropriation of exactly the same proportions; or ought ever to let the two policies lose their proper sequence, which is, appropriation first, taxation afterwards; or ought ever to decide on taxation for a longer period than that for which it votes appropriations. The only way to bring Congress to sober and conscientious ways of spending money is to insist that it assume the responsibility of raising, by its own distinctly adopted plans, the money which it spends; and the only way in which to interest public opinion in every spending vote is to put a taxing vote alongside of it. If, therefore, the financial policy of the country is to be really and effectually reformed, Congress must not be allowed to stop at recasting in some way the present tariff; it must be forced by a steady public opinion to marry the two sides of its fiscal policy, to tax as openly and as often as it spends.

There is another, an administrative, side to the subject. We can never tell whether or no we have an economical administration until appropriation and taxation be brought within sight of one another. There can be no standard of expense while there is no standard of revenue. Economy can be nothing but a matter of mere good conscience among the heads of departments so long as there is no question at all of having to ask the people for money. It will become a matter of careful and watchful policy only when it involves calling on the stockholders for fresh subscriptions.

WOODROW WILSON.

EQUALITY IN TAXATION.—COMMERCIAL UNION WITH CANADA.

By Professor Anson D. Morse, of Amherst College.

1. "*It being generally conceded that Congress must cut off some existing sources of revenue, * * * in what way should the reductions be made and upon what governing considerations?*"

The "governing consideration" should be, I think, to bring the national revenue system into accord with the maxim that "the subjects of every state ought to contribute towards the support of the government as nearly as possible in proportion to their respective abilities."

By far the larger part of the national revenue is raised on articles in common use, such as sugar, rice, fruits, and the products of wool, or on articles like tobacco, beer, and whiskey, the use of which is more common among the poor than the rich.

Is this inequality a hardship? Conclusions based on *per capita* apportionments are misleading, for the proper unit on which to base calculations is not the individual but the family. It is those wage earners who provide for large families on whom the burden of these taxes, whatever it may be, must rest most heavily; and it is towards this class in particular that public policy ought to be not only just, but humanely considerate. Perhaps the fairest way of determining the question is to find out how the expenditures of the poor are affected by the taxes on some articles of common use. According to the American standard of living, sugar is one of the "necessaries." In well-to do families its cost considerably exceeds that of flour. It is, in fact, one of the heavy items of family expenditure. In order to have a basis of fact for conclusions, I have ascertained the outlay for sugar made by five families of the town in which I live :

1.	Six persons	- -	$47.00
2.	Four "	- - -	21.00
3.	Six "	- - -	17.50
4.	Four "	- - -	27.00
5.	Five "	- - -	26.00

All these own comfortable homes, but derive their support in the main from wages. All are thrifty, and ambitious to educate their children. 1 and 2 are the families of skilled laborers; 3, 4 and 5 of unskilled, whose highest wages are $1.50 *per diem*. Except in the case of (1) the expenditure is considerably less than in families of like numbers but of larger means If we estimate that portion of the price of sugar due to the tax at forty per cent :

(1) pays - - - - $18.80
(2) "   - - - - - 8.40
(3) "   - - - -   7.00
(4) "   - - - - - 10.80
(5) " - - - -   10.40

The average is $11.08, an amount which families dependent on wages must feel as a serious addition to their necessary expenditures. The share of state, county, and town taxes of

(1) is - - - - - $12.83
(2) " - - - -   15.24
(3) " - - - - - 7.77
(4) " - - - -   9.65
(5) " - - - - - 12.64

In two cases the sugar tax exceeds all these other taxes. The average is $11.82, or .74 greater than the average sugar tax. It is evident that in the case of larger and less thrifty families, which do not own their homes, the sugar tax must considerably exceed what is assessed by state, county, and town. The only risk of error in the above calculations lies in the assumption of forty per cent as the portion of the price due to national taxation. The figures can easily be corrected if that estimate should prove either too high or too low.

The enhanced cost of the products of wool must also be a heavy burden to the poor. Owing to the nature of our climate, these products must always constitute one of the largest items of necessary expenditure. A family may, without injury to health, economize closely in the use of sugar, but to do so in the case of woolens would not only sacrifice comfort but endanger health. Moreover, it is the extremely poor whose dependence upon them is greatest. Their very poverty deprives them of other defences against the cold, such as well constructed houses, abundance of fuel, and nutritious food. It would seem as if humanity as well as justice requires the abolition of all taxes which increase the cost of the products of wool and of articles of food in common use.

But it is objected that to abolish the duties on sugar, wools, and woollens, is to deprive important industries of needed protection. Mr. Sherman has suggested a reduction of the duty on sugar and an equivalent bounty to the American producer. Why not abolish the duty altogether and give a bounty large enough to give the requisite encouragement? This would enable the consumer to obtain sugar at the lowest natural cost, and the producers, both employers and employed, to continue their production on the same terms as before. If the fund for the payment of the bounties should be raised so that the taxed should pay in proportion to their respective abilities, the chief reproach of the protective system, namely, the inequality of its burdens, would be done away. Why not extend the plan so as to include rice, fruit, fish, wool and woollens, and, indeed, all commodities in common use? Why not extend it to all industries that deserve protection?

It is true that the cost of protection would in this way be revealed. But why not reveal it? The people pay for it—why not let them know how much they pay? The people submit willingly enough to justly levied taxation for justifiable objects. The foremost advocates of protection allege that it is a national system established for the promotion of the welfare, not of a particular interest, class, or locality, but of the nation as a whole. But if the national good requires that a given industry or set of industries receive public aid, then every citizen should contribute to this, not in proportion to his wants, but in proportion to his means. In so doing, he would not suffer injustice, and his course as a citizen would be more intelligent and patriotic than under a system which takes his property by stealth, and apportions what it levies in a grossly unequal way.

To oppose bounties as a method of encouraging home industries would seem to imply distrust either of the protective system or of the people. To contend that the laborer is the one chiefly benefited by protection, and that he therefore should pay the larger part of its cost, is, even if the premise be admitted, as irrational as it would be for Massachussetts to say that because the very poor receive the benefit of the public charities, they must bear the cost.

Direct taxes justly apportioned should take the place of the existing unequal indirect ones. A distinguished advocate of protection has recently said, "The genius of our scheme of general government and the spirit of our people are hostile to direct taxation for national affairs. The federal tax-gatherer has always provoked friction and lawlessness." This I believe is altogether erroneous. The federal tax-gatherer has never provoked lawlessness except when collecting excise duties, which are forms of indirect taxation. The system of indirect taxation has continued so long partly because inherited, and partly because the people have not yet become conscious of its injustice.

In regard to the taxes on whiskey, malt liquors, and tobacco, the case is more complex. The inequality is even greater than in the previous cases; but as offset to this, it is claimed that these commodities are injurious and that the taxes lessen the consumption. It seems necessary to concede that the commodities in question are injurious. But do the national taxes add enough to their cost to sensibly lessen their use? It is, of course, conceivable that much higher rates would do so: but the question relates to present rates, the original design of which was revenue and not decrease of consumption. In answering the question, it is necessary to remember that the appetites for tobacco and liquors are usually formed under circumstances which are unfavorable to the exercise of prudential motives, and that these appetites, after becoming established, are almost as imperious,— in many cases are even more imperious,—than the natural appetites. If, notwithstanding the considerations just mentioned, it should still seem clear that these taxes do lessen the consumption of these injurious commodities, the further question would arise whether the good thus obtained compensates for the unavoidable and very considerable evils incident to the inequality of this species of taxation. It cannot be denied that these taxes do increase the poverty of the poorest classes, and that the consequent increase of suffering is borne not so much by the taxpayer in person as by his family. His self-indulgence may not be checked, but the share of his wife and children in the comforts and "higher goods" of life must thereby be lessened materially. The natural conclusion in respect to each of these taxes is that unless it can be shown to diminish in a considerable degree the use of the commodity to which it relates, it should, because of its inherent injustice, be altogether abolished.

Some of the friends of free trade or of tariff reform are inclined to retain the taxes just considered, as a leverage by which to overthrow the protective system. On the other hand, many of the friends of protection, while upholding these taxes, are willing to sacrifice one or all of them in order to strengthen their favorite system. It would seem as if each species of taxation should stand or fall on its own merits. A settlement reached in any other way can be neither just nor satisfactory.

II.

"*In a policy for the more immediate future should we contemplate the special encouragement of trade with Canada?*"

If tariff obstructions were removed, Canada would furnish a better market for our manufactures than is now the case. Her products would sensibly lessen the cost of lumber and of some articles of food in the United States, and would check the too rapid destruction of our forests. It would also open to the northern sections of New York, Vermont, and New Hampshire, the markets of the Canadian cities.

If a line were drawn from Portland, Me., to some point in the northwest corner of Washington Territory, keeping just far enough south of the Canadian boundary to include a population equal to that of the Dominion and Newfoundland, and we should then ask ourselves whether it would promote the economic welfare of the people of this narrow but immensely extended belt, or of the people of the main division of the United States, to set up custom house barriers between them, very few would maintain the affirmative. It is clear enough that certain impoverishing influences would begin to operate. The people of each section in buying and selling would find themselves excluded from the best markets. Rochester and Buffalo would have to deal with Portland instead of New York. In order to create home markets and diversify industries in the northern sections heavy taxes in the form of protective duties would be laid, and these would divert labor and capital to relatively unprofitable employments. Probably most will agree that in the case supposed, protection (looking solely at its economic results) would hurt the larger section and cripple the smaller. But in what essential respect does this case differ from that between Canada and the United States? If our revolutionary ancestors had succeeded in their efforts to induce Canada to make common cause with the thirteen colonies, or if the hopes of annexing Canada by conquest entertained by many Americans in 1812 had been realized, we would now be approving free trade between the provinces and the United States, as we do approve it between New York and New England.

But the political side of our relation to Canada is more important than the commercial. There are strong grounds for the view that Canadians and Americans should come into political unity. The British Canadians are our near kinsmen. In character and institutions they and we are essentially one. The differences between them and us are of degree—they being the more conservative; or else they are artificial, based on jealousies and contentions which ought never to have arisen.

In looking at a map of North America it is difficult to believe that the entire population of the Dominion, together with Newfoundland, does not exceed that of the State of New York. For a long time to come, inhabited Canada must consist of a narrow immensely extended border-land—a situation highly unfavorable to real economic and political independence. The natural markets of the Canadians are in the United States, and the traffic of Canada should move on lines running more nearly north and south than east and west. The attempt to reverse this natural order explains the unfortunate financial condition of Canada. Moreover, the British Canadians are not solving the French problem. The province of Quebec breaks British Canada in two, and in the race contest within the province the French more than hold their own. Indeed, it is clear that New England is doing more than British Canada to Anglo Americanize the Canadian French.

What useful or honorable thing can be named that Canada cannot better accomplish in full union with the United States, than in trying to maintain an independent career? There is nothing desirable signified by the term Canadian that is not also signified by the term American, and the latter has a certain additional significance which our neighbors need greatly to appropriate. Outside of the American Union, Canada must remain essentially provincial. Many of her more enterprising and ambitious inhabitants will be drawn to the United States, and among these some of her most gifted sons.

To the United States, union with Canada is in every way desirable; the advantages in a military and commercial point of view are sufficiently obvious. Moreover, the conservatism of the Canadians would be an element of strength in the national life.

But what commercial policy is most likely to secure union? Restrictions might be effective if economic considerations alone determined the political conduct of peoples. But they do not. Least of all do they in the case of a high-minded and spirited people. The relation between Canada and the United States is in many respects analogous to that which used to subsist between England and Scotland. But it should be remembered that all efforts on the part of England to coerce Scotland served only to defer union and make it more difficult. If union with Canada ever comes, it should be in obedience to her wish as well as ours. The readiest way to create such a wish is to pursue a policy which recognizes the essential oneness of the two peoples. But even if we should not desire union, our true policy is not to drain but to develop Canada.

ANSON D. MORSE.

A GENERAL VIEW.

By Chancellor Irving J. Manatt, of the University of Nebraska.

I have no claim to speak as a specialist on the difficult problems of taxation, but as you ask for conclusions rather than arguments, here are mine :

1. The surplus should be reduced by a thorough revision of the tariff, with constant reference to the sparing of the weak rather than the strengthening of the strong. Such revision can only be worked out by men who have mastered the complicated calculus of good and evil presented in the tariff as it is, and whose view commands the whole field of industry and commerce, not only at home but the world over. The very difficulty of the task commends free trade to many as the only easy way out. But an abandonment of the protective principles offhand and outright would probably cause greater evils than it would cure.

2. The only wise method with the public debt is the method of extinction. A national debt is a servitude on every tax-payer; every argument against getting on a shopkeeper's books, or mortgaging a farm, is as valid for the

state as for the individual. Provision for a more rapid payment of the debt, as clearly demanded by public policy, will at the same time assist in settling the surplus question. In this connection the redemption of the greenback, as urged by Secretary Manning, is well worth considering.

3. Close commercial relations among all the American states are eminently desirable. This continent can take care of itself at a pinch, and, for the present at least, feed the world. Canada and Mexico are already linked with us by great railway systems; the South American states we ought to bind to us by a strong merchant marine. Subsidies are odious; but if there is no other way to repair the ruin wrought upon our maritime commerce during the war, and not half paid for, in any far-reaching view of the matter, by the bagetelle awarded at Geneva, the end may justify even such means. A general reciprocity arrangement, including at least all the independent American states, is to be desired, both as an end in itself and as one in the long series of experiments which must go before any radical treatment of our revenue system.

4. Protection must ultimately give way to free trade—and the millennium.

IRVING J. MANATT.

STEAMSHIP SUBSIDIES AS A MEANS OF REDUCING THE SURPLUS.

By Professor Arthur T. Hadley, of Yale College.

The United States has in two instances tried the policy of steamship subsidies on a large scale: with the Collins Line in 1850–1858, and with the Pacific Mail in 1865–1875. In neither case was the result satisfactory.

The subsidy to the Collins Line was in large measure due to the efforts of Mr. King, of Georgia, for some time chairman of the House Committee on Naval Affairs. As early as 1841, only two years after the first contract of the English government with Samuel Cunard, he urged the United States to follow the example of England. The first act of Congress on the subject was passed in 1845; the amounts devoted to the payment of steamship lines were gradually increased until 1852, when they amounted to nearly $2,000,000 annually. At the close of that year there were American steamship lines running from New York to Liverpool, Havre, and Bremen; also from various American ports to the West Indies and the Isthmus of Panama, with connections thence to Oregon.

Much the most important of these enterprises

was the Collins Line, which made fortnightly trips from New York to Liverpool, for which it received a subsidy of $858,000. The history of this line is an instructive one, because it shows clearly the dangers of the subsidy system even under the most favorable circumstances. The boats were designed, built and managed by thoroughly competent men. They were the finest specimens of steamship construction then existing; they were probably the best sea-going wooden steamships which have ever been built. They were much more comfortable and much faster than the English boats with which they came into competition; and though the Cunard line was forced by the influence of their American rivals to build newer and better boats than they had before, they were far from equalling the Collins Line in speed or comfort. Nor was the American Line dishonestly managed. Mr. Collins was largely influenced by patriotic motives. So far from making any money out of his connection with this enterprise, it ultimately caused his financial ruin.

But the fact that there was no intentional dishonesty makes the absence of good economy all the more apparent. The managers believed that they had the public treasury to fall back upon. They indulged in all sorts of expenditures, necessary and unnecessary. Changes were made while the vessels were in process of construction which greatly increased their cost, in many cases without corresponding advantage. The capital stock was insufficient. The company was heavily in debt from the first. The care in management, which was the only thing that could have enabled them to carry this load of debt, was altogether wanting. If any one desired an illustration of the danger of paralyzing individual thrift by government aid, he could hardly find a better one than the early history of the Collins Line. Under such circumstances the apparent prosperity of the business could not last long. The rage for making fast passages rather than safe ones occasioned the loss of two steamers; a change of feeling in Congress caused the subsidy to be withdrawn, and the company was found to have nothing left to stand on.

The Pacific Mail had a much longer life; but its history was in many respects worse than that of the Collins Line. It was less harmed by the discontinuance of the earlier subsidies in 1858 than by the renewal of the policy in 1865. The $500,000 a year which was paid them for their China service by the contract of 1865 proved but a poor compensation for the unsound methods which were introduced into the management —in part, apparently, as the result of that contract. Up to 1865 the Pacific Mail had been a sound concern. Its shares stood above par. After that it fell into the hands of speculators;

it lost nine vessels in as many years; its shares dropped below 40. An additional subsidy of another half million was voted in 1872. But the company was unable to get the new vessels ready for service within the time stipulated; and while the government was hesitating what to do, a series of disclosures showed that the contract of 1872 had been obtained by wholesale corruption. Public opinion was strongly aroused against the system. The contracts of 1865 were allowed to expire and were not renewed. It was felt that the trade which had been encouraged had not been that of merchants in China, but of speculators and lobbyists at home.

Such facts as these furnish a strong argument against the attempt to build up an American steam marine by means of subsidies. But there are special circumstances which render the lesson doubly important at the present time.

In the first place, the difficulties of building up an American carrying trade in this manner to-day are exceptionally great. The cost of ships in America is greater than it is elsewhere. No foreign built ship is allowed to carry the American flag. Our ship-owners are thus compelled to buy in a dear market, and then compete on even terms with those whose plant is cheaper. But this is not all. Even if we were allowed, by a change in the navigation laws, to buy our ships wherever we pleased, we should not be on an equality with our competitors in this matter. In order that American capital may be attracted into the foreign carrying trade, it is necessary that the rate of interest obtainable in that business should be about as high as that which can be had in other lines of business which offer chances for investment. That is not the case at the present time. Shipping profits have been cut down by large investments of European capital, artificially stimulated by subsidies. They have been so much cut down that there has been for two or three years practically no money to be made in the business.

If the current rate of interest in France on business ventures of a certain class is 5 per cent, and in America 7 per cent, America cannot compete with France on equal terms in that business, unless she has a special advantage in the conduct of the business equal to 2 per cent on the invested capital. Forty years ago we had such an advantage, on account of our superior facilities for building ships and superior skill in sailing them. To-day both of those advantages have been neutralized. Iron has been substituted for wood, steam for sail. Nothing short of a subsidy equal to the difference in current rates of profit in the two countries would put us on an equality in this matter; and that would only do it in case France gave no subsidies at all. But France does give subsidies, on a very large scale; so large as to have stimulated an overproduction of French ships, which has done the French nation much more harm than good. To accomplish anything effective, we should have to counterbalance the difference in the rate of profit, and the French subsidies put together. Were this done, we should doubtless have a great many foreign steamship lines of our own; but they would be running for the subsidy rather than for the trade.

There is a tradition that "trade follows the flag"; that where our ships run we shall develop a trade. This may have been true before the invention of the telegraph, when the cargo was so often a matter of private enterprise on the part of the ship-owner. But there can be no doubt that it is every day less and less true; and it is probably farthest from the truth on those lines of communication where subsidized steamships would be likely to run. The notion that such lines would act as drummers for New York houses has very little basis in fact.

If, under this condition of things, we are asked to grant steamship subsidies as a patriotic way of getting rid of the surplus, the presumption is strongly against the wisdom of any such policy. In all the affairs of life, whether public or private, it is a dangerous thing to spend money simply because you have it. It is almost certain that such money will be unwisely spent.

This is conspicuously true of Government expenditures. The really wise ones have not been made where an overflowing public treasury was used to help individual enterprise, but where some specific need was felt, and the government set about to have that need met in the most efficient way.

England has at times given large steamship subsidies, but she has done it on business principles. It was a political necessity for her to have communication with her colonies, and to have steamships which could furnish her with a naval reserve, and a transport service in case of war. In order to do this she had to pay for it. She tried to pay as little as she could for the service rendered; but she could not, without political suicide, dispense with such service. She had the same reasons for subsidizing steamships that we have for maintaining postal communication on lines which do not pay. It was the same reason which has led Germany and Russia to build military railroads, or which led us to grant liberal aid to the Union Pacific in 1862 and 1864. In all these cases, it was a matter of business for the government to secure its end. The fact that the returns could not all be measured in dollars and cents did not prevent its being sound business policy. In fact, it furnished a strong reason why the government might properly make the expenditure, because there was an advantage to be gained of which individual enterprise could not reap the benefit.

But where subsidies have been given, as has been recently the case in France, or as was done in America in the instances already described, as a means of encouraging private commercial enterprise, it has not proved good business policy. It has caused waste instead of economy, loss rather than gain; it has not proved a source of naval strength or commercial prosperity for the nation which has adopted it. It has turned out to be simply an inducement to extravagance.

It is undoubtedly desirable to reduce the treasury surplus; but why? Just because it offers a temptation to extravagant uses of the money. To make the existence of such a surplus a justification for subsidies is simply to court the evil of which we are afraid. If we spend our money recklessly, we shall not have so much left to spend, and in that way the immediate danger may be diminished; but meantime we shall have done the very harm which we wished to avoid. More than this, we shall have laid the foundation for future evil of the same sort; for any such lavish expenditure of money conceals the need of wise measures to prevent its accumulation.

The existence of a surplus creates a presumption that if subsidies are granted at all they will be granted unwisely. If the surplus is made an avowed reason for granting them, this presumption becomes overwhelming. If the policy should be adopted under the influence of such arguments, we must be prepared to see it at its worst.

ARTHUR T. HADLEY.

THE IMMEDIATE TASK. — PROTECTION AND AMERICAN AGRICULTURE.

By President Francis A. Walker, of the Massachusetts Institute of Technology.

THE IMMEDIATE TASK.

Many of those with whom the writer has been accustomed to act or to sympathise, on the question of tariff duties, have seemed disposed, during the past few months, both before the meeting of Congress and since the session began, to regard the existence of the surplus as a weapon properly to be used in compelling a revision of the tariff; if not a general reduction of duties, then the placing upon the free list of certain articles, e.g., wool, lumber, salt, coal, iron, etc., which are peculiarly obnoxious as the subjects of " protective " legislation. These persons have held, not only that the existence of a large excess of revenue above the legitimate wants of the government, and even above its capacity for wanton and wasteful expenditure, must give great logical force to the demands for tariff reduction, but also that the apprehensions felt regarding the industrial and financial effects of largely and rapidly increasing the funds in the treasury must bring a strong moral and political pressure upon Congress, making it easier to carry the desired scheme of tariff revision and reduction than if such a financial situation did not exist ; perhaps making it possible to do this where it would have been impossible otherwise, in the nearly equal division of Congress on the tariff, and the thorough demoralization of both parties regarding this issue.

I even think that some of these persons have regarded the occurrence of this overwhelming reason for tariff reform as almost "providential" in securing a degree of public attention to the subject, and imparting an urgency to the parliamentary discussion of it, far in advance of what has hitherto been or would otherwise be.

I confess that while entertaining no distrust of the disinterested and patriotic purposes of these gentlemen, it has seemed and still seems to me untimely and dangerous to use the surplus as a means of getting leverage for the reform of the tariff. The surplus is so prolific a source of political corruption, its existence and rapid increase constitute so grave a menace to our industrial and financial integrity, as to make it the first duty of all Congressmen, whether democrats or republicans, whether protectionists or free traders, to join together, as against a common enemy, to put together immediately some bill for greatly reducing the revenue, alike without sacrificing their individual convictions on the general question, and without seeking through such legislation to obtain any advantage for their respective party with reference to the struggle still to come over the tariff.

It has seemed to me that patriotic men, of both parties, might have come together in December, or might come together now, and in a week, nay, in a single day, make up a measure which would strike off eighty or a hundred millions of unnecessary revenue, without raising any difficult question weakening the position of either party on the main issue, or alienating enough votes to sustain a demand for the yeas and nays.

PROTECTION AND AMERICAN AGRICULTURE.[*]

The question of Protection, as against Freedom of Production—not, as it is commonly stated, against Freedom of Trade—is rarely discussed, on both sides, upon purely economic principles; perhaps has never been, in an actual instance, decided without the intermixture of political or social considerations.

The arguments of those who have favored the policy of so far limiting the territorial division of labor as to constitute industrial entities corresponding to existing political entities (which I take to be the real intent of what is called pro-

---

[*] By permission of Gen. Walker this discussion of the relation of the protective system to American agriculture is reprinted from the revised edition of his "Political Economy" (New York, 1887).

tection), have been of every degree of vagueness; but it seems to me that the confusion of the public mind need not have existed, at least to so great an extent, had not the professional economists taken an unjustifiable lofty attitude on this subject, practically refusing to argue the question at all as one of national expediency, contenting themselves with occupying the high ground of *Laissez Faire*.

Now, that doctrine, although established by the older economists to their own satisfaction, as containing a principle of universal application, and thus deemed by them a conclusive answer to all arguments especially directed to justify restrictions upon international trade, has never been accepted, in the fulness of significance by them given it, throughout any wide constituency, nor by any large proportion of the educated classes, not even generally by publicists, or statesmen, or men of affairs.

Thus, when factory legislation was first proposed in England, nearly the whole body of professional economists opposed any interference with the freedom of contract respecting labor. They asserted the entire competence of the laboring classes to protect their own interests. They declared that interference on behalf of the laboring classes could only be mischievous in the long run to the laborers themselves. They put themselves on record in the most formal manner against all measures of restriction upon factory and workshop labor. They cast in their lot with the opposition to this class of legislation, and staked the reputation and influence of political economy upon their being right in this matter.

Had they won upon that issue, had the results of the factory acts been proved deleterious to the interests of the working classes themselves, or even to the industrial power of the kingdom, it would have been a rare triumph for the economists, and their influence would have been greatly strengthened. But it did not turn out so. Although in the first instance, that of the act of 1802, Sir Robert Peel, the elder, had been so solicitous not to violate the principle of the self-sufficiency of labor that he made the bill apply only to apprentices, the wards of the State, the political rightfulness and the economic expediency of regulating the contract for labor so grew upon the public mind of England that act after act extended the supervision of the State over factory and workshop, until the policy of restriction had vindicated itself to the complete satisfaction of the working classes, even, in the main, of the master class themselves, and of the statesmen of the kingdom and publicists almost without exception.

The fact that in the controversy over the factory acts the economists of the *laissez-faire* school are proved to have been in the wrong, does not show, or go to show, that they were wrong in their opposition to laws in restraint of international commerce. It does not even create a presumption to that effect.

Although the necessity of making exceptions to the rule of freedom of individual action has been established as completely in respect to industry as in respect to politics, freedom of action is yet so far the condition of health and power and growth in the field alike of politics and of industry, that those who propose to make exceptions in either are bound to show cause for every such exception. A heavy burden of proof rests upon them. Their case is to be made, and made against a powerful presumption in favor of liberty, as that condition which hath the promise not only of that which now is, but, in a higher degree, of that which is to come. There is not, and there can never be, any positive virtue in restraint. Its only office for good is to prevent waste and save the misdirection of energy. There is no life in it, and no force can come out of it.

That which is called "protection" operates only by restraint; it has and can have neither creative power nor healing efficacy. All the energy that is to produce wealth exists before it and without respect to it; and just to the extent to which protection operates at all, it operates by impairing that energy and reducing the sum of wealth that might be produced if protection did not exist.

I say, that might be produced, not that *would* be produced. The latter point may fairly be disputed between the free trader, who should rather be called the free producer, and the advocate of the system of restricted production. The force of the steam at the piston-head is less than the force of the steam in the boiler, less by all that is necessary to conduct it thither from the boiler; yet it is the force of the steam at the piston-head, and not where it is generated, which moves the wheels of the engine. The harness hampers the movements of the horse; but it is the harnessed horse that draws the load. Discipline operates directly to reduce the sum of the impulses by which soldiers are actuated, and by consequence to reduce their individual energy; but a disciplined army will defeat a mob of many times its own numbers.

If the protectionist can show that restraints imposed by law upon the industrial action of his countrymen, or the men of any country he chooses to take for the purposes of the debate, have the effect, not, indeed, to generate productive force, but to direct the productive force generated by human wants setting in motion human labor, with a better actual result than under the rule of freedom, he will make his case. But this is to be proved, not taken for granted; and it is to be proved only by sound and serious argument, not by strenuous assertion and senseless clamor.

* * * * * * * *

It will readily appear that the protectionist writers have a difficult task in establishing the necessity of drawing the lines of industrial circumvallation along the boundaries of empire.

Take the United States for example. Here are thirty-eight states, trading among themselves with the utmost activity, the exchange of commodities and services being as free as the movements of the air; and in this freedom all good citizens rejoice; but this condition of things is made, by the doctrine under examination, to be dependent entirely upon the political relations of these states. Were they under different governments, the exchange of commodities and services which now promotes the general wealth and the general welfare would be fraught with mischief and possible ruin.

It is, of course, possible that some new analysis of the conditions of production may yet disclose the law which thus makes trade within the limits of sovereignty beneficial, and trade across the boundaries of separate states deleterious to one or both parties; but thus far, assertion coupled with vituperation has taken the place of the analysis required.

In the Old World, the argument for protection

is based on the importance of protecting the industrially weak against the industrially strong; and I am not certain that something might not be said for this. Russia strives to protect her labor against the better paid labor of Germany; Germany, in turn, strives to protect her labor against the vastly better paid labor of England. Among all fully settled countries, the rule, without exception so far as I am aware, is that that country in which the higher wages are paid offers its products at lower prices than the competing products of countries where the lower wages are paid

In the United States, however, the argument for protection has based itself on the assumed necessity of protecting the strong against the weak. In Australia and Canada it is the same. It is alleged to be necessary to the maintenance of the high wages prevailing in these countries, that the products of the "pauper labor of Europe" shall not be sold freely in their markets.

Why is it that the plea of those who desire to check the extension of the division of labor on the lines of nationality, suddenly changes as they pass from old and fully settled countries to countries but recently, and perhaps still but partially, occupied and cultivated?

The explanation is found in the fact that the populations of what we call "new countries," that is, countries where an inadequate population is applying progressively to fresh fields advanced methods and machinery, possess an immense advantage in the conditions of living over the populations of "old countries," where the land has long been fully occupied, where the capabilities of the soil, even on fields of small natural productiveness, are heavily taxed to furnish subsistence to the inhabitants, and where systematic, continuous manuring has to be practiced in order to keep the land in condition.

The enormous profit of cultivating the virgin soil without the need of artificial fertilization, and the abundance of food and other necessaries of life enjoyed by the agricultural class, have tended continually to disparage the mechanical industries in the eyes alike of the American capitalist and of the American laborer.

It has been the competition of the farm with the shop which has, from the first, most effectually retarded the growth of manufactures in the United States. A population which is privileged to live upon a virgin soil, cultivating only the choicest fields, and cropping these through a succession of years without returning anything to the land, can live in plenty. If that population possess the added advantage of great skill in the use of tools, and great adroitness in meeting the large and the little exigencies of the occupation and the cultivation of the soil, the fruits of agriculture will still further be greatly increased. The dietary of an American farmer, cultivating his own land with the aid of his growing sons, would amaze a peasant from any portion of Europe. An abundance of nutritious food is and has been ever since the Revolutionary period, the sure condition of the life of the agriculturist in the United States. It was not with our fathers, even in New England, a struggle for the necessaries of life, but for social decencies and what, in any old country, would have been called luxuries.

Now, the mode of living on the part of the agricultural population has necessarily set a minimum standard of wages for mechanical labor. With an abundance of cheap land, with a population facile to the last degree in making change of avocation and of residence, few able-bodied men are likely to be drawn into factories and shops on terms which imply a meaner subsistence than that secured in the cultivation of the soil.

There are certain classes of mechanical pursuits, however, which by their nature secure to those who follow them a minimum remuneration fully up to the standard of the agricultural wages of the region. Such, for instance, are the trades of carpenter, blacksmith, and mason, in which the work is of a kind which can only be done upon the spot. The house cannot be built abroad and imported for the farmer's use; the wagon must be mended near the place where it broke down; the horse must be shod, the tools sharpened by the artisans of the neighborhood. If, then, the farmer will have such services performed, he must admit those who perform them to share his own abundance; he must pay wages or prices which will attract men, and those by necessity men exceptionally intelligent and skilful, into those trades. Hence, we find the mason, the blacksmith, the plumber, the carpenter, the house-painter, the cobbler, in every part of the United States, receiving wages which bear no relation whatever to the wages paid for the same class of services in other countries, but which stand in a very exact relation to the rewards of agricultural labor here.

Nor has it ever been found necessary to encourage or stimulate these trades for the good of the country. What statesman ever introduced into Congress a bill intended to increase the number of carpenters or blacksmiths, or to enhance their wages?

But, again, there are certain classes of services of a personal or professional nature, which have also secured for those rendering them a participation in the abundance enjoyed by the tillers of the soil in the same region. The remuneration received by the members of these classes, whether called the wages of domestic servants or the fees of physicians and lawyers, or the salaries of schoolmasters and clergymen, or the profits of retail trade, has been out of all relation to the remuneration of similar services in other countries, and has amounted to just what I have termed it, *a participation in the abundance enjoyed by the agricultural population.* Since these services could only be performed upon the spot, the agriculturists have been obliged, if they would have the services rendered, to pay for them, out of the large surplus of their own produce, at least enough to make these professions and avocations equally desirable with their own, uncertainty of result, loss of time in preparation, expense of education and training, healthfulness and agreeableness of work, etc., being taken into account ; and since the agricultural classes have desired that these services should be performed, and have been willing to pay for them on the scale indicated, there has never been any call for Congressional action to secure the requisite number of lawyers, physicians, clergymen, schoolmasters, domestic servants, or retail tradesmen.

But now we note that there are still other important classes of services to be rendered, respecting which the rule changes. The remuneration of the persons rendering these services no longer has reference to the abundance of agricultural production in the several sections of the United States; is no longer irrespective of the remuneration of similar classes elsewhere. These persons are not, necessarily, admitted to a participation in the fruits of American agriculture.

The services referred to are such as can be performed without respect to the location of the consumer of the product. They are nearly identical with what we call in the technical sense of the term, manufactures.

Whenever the American farmer wants a pane of glass set, or a pair of boots mended, or a horse shod, he must pay some one, his neighbor, enough for doing the job to keep him in his trade, and to keep him out of agriculture, in the face of the great advantages of tilling the soil, in New York, or Ohio, or Dakota, or wherever else the farmer in question may live; but how much he shall pay the man who *makes* the pane of glass or the pair of boots or the set of horse-shoes, will depend upon the advantages of tilling the soil, not where he himself lives, but where the maker of the horse-shoes, the boots, or the glass may live.

If he will have the work done he must pay some one, somewhere, enough to keep him in his trade and out of agriculture; but not necessarily out of New York agriculture, or Ohio agriculture, or Dakota agriculture; but perhaps out of English agriculture, or French agriculture, or

Norwegian agriculture, under the requirements of constant fertilization, deep ploughing and thorough drainage, and subject to that stringent necessity which economists express by the term "the law of Diminishing Returns."

Now, to offset and overcome the inducements to engage in agriculture, even in Merry England, is a different thing, a very different thing, from keeping a man in his trade and out of agriculture in the United States.

The American agriculturist, having large quantities of grain and meat, of cotton and tobacco left on his hands, after providing ample subsistence for his family, and even after hiring the carpenter, mason, and blacksmith, the schoolmaster, lawyer, and doctor, for as much time as he requires their respective services, and still further, after putting a good deal into farm implements and increase of stock, is desirous of obtaining with the remainder sundry articles more or less necessary to health, comfort, and decency. To him it makes no difference whether the articles he requires are made on one side of the Atlantic or on the other; but it makes a great difference what he is obliged to pay for them; how much of his surplus grain and meat, tobacco and cotton, must go to secure a certain definite satisfaction of his urgent and oft-recurring wants. If he must needs pay some one to stay out of American agriculture and do this work, his surplus will not go so far as if he were allowed to pay some one to stay out of English agriculture to do it.

But here the state enters and declares that it is socially or politically necessary that these articles, these nails, these horse-shoes, this cotton or woollen cloth, or what not, shall be made on this side of the Atlantic. That necessity the agriculturist, as consumer, cannot be expected to feel; he does not care where the things were made; he only wants them to use. He does not care who makes them; he does not even care whether they are made at all; they would answer his purpose just as well were they the gratuitous gifts of nature, spontaneous fruits of the soil, or the sea, or the sky. Whatever his own economic theories may be, he will, as purchaser, every time select the cheapest article which will precisely answer his need. He will not, of his own motion, pay more for an article because it is made on his side of the Atlantic than he could get an equally good article for, bearing the brand of Sheffield or Birmingham or Manchester. But if the state says he must, he must; and consequently the American maker of this article is by force of law admitted to a participation in the abundance enjoyed by the American agricultural class. The tiller of the soil is now compelled, by the ordinance of the state, to share his bread and meal with the maker of nails or horse-shoes, of cotton or of woollen cloth, just as he was before compelled by the ordinance of Nature to share his bread and meat with the blacksmith, carpenter and mason, the schoolmaster, lawyer and doctor.

It is perfectly true, therefore, as the protectionist asserts, that a tariff of customs duties upon foreign goods imported into new countries tends to create and maintain high rates of wages in the factory industries. But for protective duties, those articles which, in their nature, can be readily and cheaply transported will be produced predominantly in countries where the minimum standard of mechanical wages is set by agricultural conditions far less favorable than those which obtain in the United States and Canada, or in Australia.

But while the law thus can and does create high rates of wages in factory industries, it does not and it cannot create the wealth out of which that excess of manufacturing wages over those of older countries is paid. That wealth is created by the labor and capital employed in the cultivation of the soil.

FRANCIS A. WALKER.

THE TARIFF AND THE WESTERN FARMER.

By Professor James H. Canfield, of the University of Kansas

I am asked to express in, say, two thousand words, my opinion of the relations of the protective system to Western development and to the agricultural interests of these Missouri Valley States. That means, necessarily, more assertion than carefully developed argument; an abrupt statement, so compressed as to be exceedingly liable to misconception. In spite of this, I cheerfully comply with the request and cast in my mite. Let it be accepted as coming not from an "economist," but from one whose ten years in the business world brought him into close contact with practical affairs in the West, thus presenting the opportunities for observation under which this judgment was formed.

The general effect of the protective system on Western development and upon our agricultural interests is detrimental and repressive. We are handicapped at the beginning of the race, and heavy weighted clear through to the end. That we have made rapid advancement goes without saying; we simply cannot help this, with the constant influx of fresh blood, much of it the best that the country affords. That the tariff tax has been our only enemy is not true; we have all the failings and shortcomings of mankind, and must make the usual struggle against nature both within and without ourselves. But at every step we have been obliged to overcome tariff obstacles; and some of these have been so great as to prove insurmountable to the weaker folk who have tried to "grow up with the country," and have painfully failed.

Take Kansas as a fairly typical state. It has just completed the first quarter century of its existence. During the four years of civil strife it was subjected to all the terrible waste and strain of border war. Since peace came, it has been compelled to wrestle with grasshoppers and with drouth. Its water supply is small, and its timber very inadequate. It is at a great distance from those central markets, those points of storage, where the prices of most of its exports are determined. Rival Western States have left no stone unturned to direct from it both population and capital. It has a fine climate, a wonderfully fertile soil, and a commanding geographical position. Consider very briefly what was needed that it might most readily and surely rise in material well-being and in influence and power.

First, we needed cheap lumber to make shelter for man and beast. But the tariff on lumber has beyond question proved a most burdensome tax; the amount, by most careful calculation, reaching not less than a half million of dollars per annum for each of the last five years, and only less in previous years in proportion to the population. So clearly has this been seen that our Legislature, though strongly partisan, a few years ago by a joint resolution asked that lumber be put on the free list. The tribute which we pay is not only expensive, but it is absurd, because it cannot by any stretch of language be said to "build up an industry;" it is inconsistent, because it puts a premium on the destruction of the forests which we are offering bounties to preserve; and it is dangerous, because the deforestation of this country is bringing with it disease and storm and ruin.

Iron has become a necessity. Its manifold uses mark the advance of civilization. But wherever we have touched it, and we have touched it a thousand times each day, we found —not the mark of the customs officer, we could bear that cheerfully!—but the brand of the Pennsylvanian. *That* was hard!

We needed cheap methods of transportation. But up to 1883 we had paid ten millions of dollars more than we ought, more than was necessary, for the track then laid within the state; or we were trying to sustain passenger and freight rates that would pay running expenses and interest and profits on that plant. Since that year we have increased our mileage marvellously, at an extra and useless cost of not less than fifteen hundred dollars per mile. And what is true of our internal system is also true of every mile of the hundreds outside of the State which must be traversed in order to reach our leading markets or to return home.

We needed good agricultural implements, at the lowest possible prices. But one firm alone, in Wisconsin, manufacturing largely for the Western trade, paid in a single year more than thirty thousand dollars increased price (tariff tax) on the iron and steel which it used. Of course, Western farmers paid it back, and with interest. In the course of time we erected flour and feed and grist mills, engaged in printing and book-binding, began to make our own furniture, went from wagon-making to building carriages, began to turn our straw into coarse paper, established little sorghum mills at occasional four-corners, a few cities were lighted with gas, one stove foundry came into successful operation; we fenced in the prairies with wire; we marked the resting places of the dead with marble. But the tax kept pace with us; and in all these, in raw materials and in machinery and in added cost of transportation, we bore at least a double tax.

We needed foundries and machine shops and

repair shops, and we even ventured to erect a few woollen mills. But these use iron and steel in machinery, pay for iron and steel in transportation rates, and in these and in the added cost of raw material pay a triple tax.

As in all new communities, we were forced to content ourselves with "domestic manufactures," and so were obliged to take the coarser and more imperfect fabrics; thus again bearing the double tax of inferior quality and superior price.

Nor could we learn that a dollar of all this went into the treasury of the national government. We were working hard; carrying the exceptional burdens inseparable from opening and improving a new country; needing help as much as Chicago did after the great fire, when the government remitted duties on all materials used in rebuilding — except lumber; trying to get houses, and food, and clothing, and schools, and churches, and books, and journeys, and all the thousand-and-one things that fill life with enjoyment and contentment; and possibly hoping to put by a little something for that inevitable "rainy day." We were taking our grain and cattle and hogs, and all that we raised, into the world's market, and selling it for whatever the world would give; and always going home with the price in our hands to buy in a market where the unseen tax collector determined the price. While carrying all the load of improvement and development, we were paying to the hidden guardian of the "American system" more than the total of all local taxes.

We were told that the money thus exacted was for the betterment of the Eastern laborers. Out of our necessities we have placed something more than twelve dollars per capita (on our entire population) in local manufactures, none of which can by any pretext be said to be protected. These had come naturally, freely, without wrangling, without legislative action — better still, without legislative corruption. We simply followed the injunction of common sense: "Seek first that which you are fitted to do, and diversity of industries will be added unto you in due season." When comparisons are instituted we find that of the whole number of our laborers in manufactures, ninety-two and one half per cent are men, four and a half per cent are children, and only three per cent are women. This means that our wives and mothers are in their homes, and that our children are in the schools. But in Massachusetts, which we have been taxed to support, only some sixty-five per cent. of such laborers are men; while Pennsylvania has thirty thousand children engaged in most constant and wearying toil. Moreover, it appears that Massachusetts pays but thirty-three dollars per annum (average wages) more than we do; and Pennsylvania, where night gangs and seven-day men abound, pays but fifteen dollars more. These differences seem but small results from such a constant drain as is made on the agricultural districts of the West. Further, the census tells us that the average wages in the eight leading "protected" industries—iron, steel, woollens, cottons, glass, silks, pottery, and carpets — is actually five dollars *less* per annum than the average wages in Kansas non-protected work; less, too, than can be earned by any farm hand in this state.

We used to be told that the industries which we were required to support were making low prices possible where otherwise there would be no competition, and we would be entirely at the mercy of "the foreigner." For a time we believed that, and even now recognize that there may be an atom of truth in the statement. But we now know that the expense has far exceeded the benefit; that competition between these "foreigners" has forced down prices abroad; that if our own prices have fallen it has simply been because the "foreigners" led in the decline and we were obliged to follow; that the law that has governed wheat has had its effect on iron and steel in spite of the protective wall; and that "trusts" and "syndicates" and all manner of nefarious combinations have been possible in this country, where they would never have been known had our ports been open.

As to the "home market" it has never come. A continually increasing per cent of our cereals has been shipped abroad, and the surplus has determined the price. And even the cry of "pauper labor" loses its force when we look eastward and see that even in pauper labor we can at last compete with the world.

And in the face of all this the Missouri Valley has prospered? In a certain way, yes. I do not think we have *created* much yet, not as much by a great deal as we should have done under freedom. There has been a vast shifting of population towards the center of the Union. Nearly all these people have brought money with them, and have expended it here. Eastern capital has flooded the state through the loan offices, and in this way most of the permanent improvements have been made. The increased population has caused a rise in land values. By this increase in values—in the great majority of cases, by actual transfer and by voluntary expatriation — land mortgages have been paid. But they still lie like a cloud over the land. Cities have been built: partly a natural growth and partly artificial. But municipal indebtedness has grown faster than the cities. With the trading class, whose taxes on the whole diffuse themselves most readily, there has been advancement. But the great mass of our population is still rural; and shut our eyes to the facts as we may, is in a depressed and deplorable condition. The most powerful and immediate cause, though not the only cause of this, I have endeavored to set forth in these hasty lines.

All observation and testimony tend to prove that the general conclusion reached is no less applicable to other great agricultural communities of the West.

JAMES H. CANFIELD.

INTERNAL TAXATION AND A REVENUE TARIFF.

By Professor Arthur Yager, of the Georgetown (Ky.) College.

In this matter of financial policy, the American Republic has at last come to the parting of the ways. The vague generalities and straddling duplicities of party platforms and the temporary expedients and procrastinations of recent Congresses will no longer suffice. A gigantic surplus, menacing the equipoise of our whole industrial system, imperiously demands a readjustment of our national finances.

That this state of affairs should have been allowed to come upon us is itself a political outrage scarcely paralleled in the history of free peoples; and it constitutes a curious commentary on the improvidence and helplessness of the partisan politics of the present day.

But the issue before the present Congress is a much broader one than the mere reduction of the revenues and consequent obviation of a surplus. The time has come for such a thorough readjustment of the whole scheme of national finance as will make the recurrence of surplus revenues impossible, and will settle our future financial policy upon some broad and permanent lines.

Our great commercial interests demand this, and our national legislature cannot discharge its duty without contributing something toward these great ends.

To accomplish these ends satisfactorily it seems to me necessary for us to choose one of two possible courses of action: In the first place we may abolish the internal revenue and the non-protective features of the tariff, and thus commit ourselves wholly and permanently to the policy of protection. Secondly, we may retain the internal revenue and accomplish the necessary reduction by such a change in the rates of duties as will gradually bring them to the revenue basis. The issue presented by the present situation clearly involves, in my opinion, the unreserved acceptance or the definite abandonment of the protective principle.

It is to be hoped that the issue will be honestly and candidly accepted by the political parties of the day. The President has set a noble example of statesmanlike courage and candor, which, if followed by the rest of our political leaders, will give us for once a political combat to be fought on the field of ideas and principles.

There are several important reasons why we should retain our internal revenue.

In the first place, these taxes are laid upon

articles which have been recognized by all nations and in all times as fit subjects of taxation. One of the earliest taxes imposed by the American government was a tax upon spirits.

The revenue collected from this source is paid by the consumers of articles which are not only not necessaries of life, but which are in many cases positively injurious to the health of those using them. The tax is therefore in the nature of a voluntary contribution to the government.

Moreover, by the abolition of the internal revenue we would confine ourselves almost entirely to one source of revenue, and that source one which, being dependent upon the volume of foreign commerce, might easily be cut off by war or other international complication. All governments should have diversified sources of revenue. No civilized country of modern times, save our own, has ever been guilty of the insane folly of relying wholly upon taxes on imports. Whenever we have done so, it has cost us dear. The war of 1812 and the civil war each brought the government to the verge of bankruptcy, because at the breaking out of hostilities in each case we were depending entirely upon tariff duties as a source of revenue.

The reduction of revenues must, therefore, come from changes in the tariff; and, for myself, I am firmly convinced that the time has come for us to begin to abandon the policy of protection.

In order to reach this conclusion it is not necessary to enter into a scientific discussion of the relative merits of free trade and protection as economic theories.

There is no doubt much of extravagant assertion and dogmatic denial on both sides. We may be permitted to hesitate to accept the sweeping claims made by enthusiastic adherents of both schools of political economy. On this point suffice it to say that the American Republic has for a hundred years enjoyed an uninterrupted and most remarkable course of industrial development; that in this hundred years we have been part of the time under a protective tariff, and part of the time under a tariff for revenue only; and that it is still an open question as to which of these epochs have been most prosperous.

To the average American mind, this plain statement of fact will appear fatal to most of the wild claims of extreme theorists on both sides.

But apart from the distinctions of economic theories, there are many practical reasons why we should, as soon as possible, lay aside the protective principle. In the first place, a protective tariff brings about an artificial state of things highly dangerous to the commercial stability of the country and corrupting to legislation. To one familiar with the gusts and passions of popular government, there is something awful in the spectacle of those great masses of capital engaged in manufacturing enterprises which seem to depend for their existence and prosperity upon an act of Congress. And the powerful and persistent influence brought to bear upon each successive Congress by these great protected interests is a serious menace to the cause of good government.

A protective tariff is, moreover, contrary to our distinctively American polity. Protection means restriction, and the political ideas of America have been from the beginning set to the march of unlimited freedom both of person and contract, of speech and trade, within and without our national boundaries. Our protective tariffs constitute the only important exception to this general policy. It is doubtless due in part to this national feeling that not one of our protective tariffs has ever been adopted as an original proposition and on its merits. The short-lived and unimportant tariff of 1842 constitutes only an apparent exception to this important statement. Speaking "bye and large," we have lived under only two epochs of genuine protection, namely 1816–1833 and 1861–1888. In both cases the protective principle was adopted in response to the demands of manufacturing interests that had grown up out of the confusion and disturbance of war, and in both cases that principle was perpetuated in part through the same powerful influence.

Lastly, a policy of protection cannot in this country be a stable policy. A glance at the history of protection in America will reveal the fact that this policy always encounters from the first serious and wide-spread opposition; that the opposition always leads to agitation for tariff reform which grows in violence and volume, causing great disturbance to the immense business interests involved; and that finally, in spite of the advantage of position, of vested interests, and money, the protectionists are defeated.

In short, an attentive study of our political history will show that protective tariffs have been begotten of war and disaster; that they have been perpetuated by persistent and powerful pleas for the protection of vested interests; and that finally, after some twenty years of constant agitation, they have been overthrown.

The tariff of 1861 seems to be following the appointed course; and if so, the time for its downfall has arrived.

ARTHUR YAGER.

A PLAN OF TARIFF REDUCTION.

By Professor Edward W. Bemis, of the Vanderbilt University.

A few things may be taken for granted. First, that the revenue should be reduced from $50,000,000 to $75,000,000. There would still be enough left for such a plan of refunding as Prof. Henry C. Adams advocated in the "Forum" for December, 1887, since the surplus this year is estimated at $113,000,000 by the Secretary of the Treasury. Enough would also be left for the purchase of the Western Union Telegraph system, which, in the writer's opinion, ought to be at once undertaken; and for such public buildings, internal improvements, and fortifications, as a wise regard for the public interest may recommend.

In the second place, this reduction must come in the internal revenue, which yielded in 1886-7 $30,108,067.13 from tobacco and $87,751,509.20 from liquors; or it must come in the tariff, which yielded $217,286,893.13; or partly in both.

Finally it should be distinctly understood that the advocate of a reduction at present in the tariff is not obliged to reject the great protectionist argument stated by Mill, and best elaborated by List in his National Economy, and Sidgwick in his Political Economy, relative to the wisdom of temporary protection to infant industries. The question is not one of immediate removal of all customs duties, which even the most pronounced free trader would deprecate as too much of a cold bath to be ventured at once; neither is it a question, such as confronted Hamilton, of formulating at the very beginning of a nation's development its economic policy.

Considering, therefore, only the issue now before the country, it seems to me clear that the reduction should be almost entirely in the tariff. There are at least two weighty reasons for leaving the internal revenue as it is. It is a tax on luxuries; and it may fairly be said in the case of liquor, and even in considerable measure of tobacco, to be a tax on vices. Such heightening of the price through taxation as will serve to restrict their use, must meet the approval of all moralists. A tax on luxuries is advocated by economists as the most in harmony with the accepted canon of taxation—that it should be proportionate to ability to pay.

The second and less familiar but none the less important reason for retaining the tax on both liquor and tobacco, is the great wisdom and almost necessity of having in our hands a machinery for revenue which we can depend upon and make more effective when some crisis, such as foreign war, shall require a sudden increase of revenue. Customs duties, from the injury to commerce by war, always decrease and almost cease when most needed, as during our civil war, when our commerce and imports were far less affected than would happen in war with foreign countries, such as may overtake us when we least expect it.

Prof. Henry C. Adams has clearly shown, in his invaluable work on Public Debts, the great losses and national danger in the wars of 1812 and 1861 from the lack at the start of an efficient internal revenue system.

Such being the reasons for retaining the internal revenue, how is it with the tariff? It here becomes necessary to develope some theory as to the reasons for protection. I will in this article admit that there may be force in some protectionist arguments, and will endeavor to consider the subject in a judicial spirit.

I believe that the results of protection are very different when applied to so-called raw materials, like the products of the mine and the forest, from what they are when applied to those industries we call manufactures, which make use of such forms of division of labor as lead to the collection of thousands in small areas. Work in producing raw materials, save in mining, is extensive, in manufactures it is intensive. One scatters men apart from each other and prevents the stimulus of social contact; the other collects men in closely settled communities. The first requires much capital and skill in organization and management; the latter requires far less of both. Of course some capital and agricultural skill is important on a farm, but no one would compare it with that needed in the management of a large cotton mill or iron foundry.

Now it seems to me that protection cannot for any length of time help the wage earner in either kind of labor. The increasing and already great mobility of labor is fast producing equality of compensation for the same service in the United States and Western Europe. It is no idle assertion, made for the sake of carrying a point, when I say that reliable statistics show that already wages in many industries, even of those where we have a tariff, are as high by the piece in England and Germany as here.

It is not denied that a tariff, by its stimulus to an industry, may attract workmen to it and very likely lead to an increased influx from Europe. But what is the gain thereby to the wage-earner? We are fast seeing the folly of Joseph Cook's desire to see our population numbered by the hundred millions, and are realizing that in happiness, as in land, we may reach a point of diminishing returns, and find that there is more comfort and civilization possible with one hundred millions or less, than with five times the number.

But I agreed to admit, as I honestly can, some force to protectionist arguments. A protective tariff does undoubtedly stimulate the industries protected, though it may not for any length of time directly raise the wages of the laborers in them. The simple question is this : Are there any great advantages that may come to the country as a whole from thus stimulating special industries ? Here we see the importance of the distinction between raw materials and manufactures. Without here claiming that a tariff is the best way of stimulating an industry, it seems to me clear that, if we admit the wisdom of protection at all, there are reasons for protecting manufactures which do not exist for protecting workers in raw material ; or if we reject the entire protectionist scheme, but yet admit, as all do, the impolicy of removing all the tariff at once, we are aided by the above distinction in deciding where reduction can best begin.

The strongest argument for protection, as Sidgwick puts it, is the need of aid to infant industries for which one country is naturally as well fitted as another, but which require large capital and great experience in the manager, and consequently may be swamped at the outset by the cut-rate competition of established firms in other countries. A case in point is that of Mr.

Williston, at Easthampton, Mass., years ago, who secured a patent by which he could manufacture thread cheaper than Coates in Great Britain, but was compelled to desist by their selling far below cost, until his smaller capital was in danger of total loss.

But this argument applies solely to manufactures and mining, since, as was shown, in these only is large capital and great managerial skill required.

Another great reason for desiring protection has usually been given as the intenser social and mental activity, the quickened life which comes to a community from a diversified industry, and particularly from manufactures. As we have seen, manufactures alone can produce this, since they alone concentrate peoples in cities and large villages where this mental stimulus leading to invention and quickened social life is most seen. Gunton, in his interesting work, "Wealth and Progress," shows the close connection between social wants and wages, and maintains, in opposition to Henry George, that not only nominal but real wages are highest in cities where rents are high and the social desires and demands greatest.

All these are strong reasons for preferring protection to manufactures rather than to raw material, and, in the writer's opinion, sufficient to induce even a moderate protectionist to favor reduction in the tariff on raw material rather than in the internal revenue. Many will prefer, as a national ideal, to see a large though scattered farming community rather than the rapid growth of cities; but evidently a change of this kind could be as much effected by tariff reduction, provided only duties on manufactures as well as on raw material were lowered, as by leaving the customs duties as they are and reducing the tax on liquor and tobacco.

If the above reasoning is accepted, we should naturally take off in whole or in part the following customs duties. Only the most important are selected, and the revenue for 1887 given:

Wool	$6,390,055	
Seeds	172,438	
Flax, Hemp and Jute	1,930,340	
Bristles	174,424	
Hops	1,329,500	— 9,996,757
Animals	$933,013	
Breadstuffs	1,075,811	
Chicory	106,672	
Fish	611,938	
Fruits and Nuts	4,214,779	
Hay	157,445	
Oils, Olive and other salad	163,648	
Meat and Dairy products	430,007	
Rice	971,455	
Salt	676,866	
Spices	66,271	
Molasses	1,496,863	
Sugar	56,507,496	
Potatoes	214,638	
Other vegetables	332,872	
Miscellaneous food products	38,560	— 67,998,334
Hides and Skins	1,329,506	
Wood, sawed	994,726	
Art Works	577,772	— 2,002,004
		$80,897,095

If we add the duty on coal and coke of $683,728, which the arbitrary methods of the anthracite coal monopoly would justify, as also the resulting benefit to manufactures, we should have $81,580,823 as the duty on the leading raw materials.

If reductions, however, are made in raw materials, corresponding reductions at least would have to be made in duties on completed products, like clothing, into which any of these entered as raw material, so that a reduction of probably over $40,000,000 more could here be made without loss to the manufacturer. But $70,000,000 is the utmost advisable reduction of the national revenue at present. Consequently a considerable protection could still be given to many of the articles just mentioned.

In order not to precipitate sudden disaster and ruin upon the Louisiana sugar planters, it might be well to adopt the suggestion of Senator Dawes, and, taking off $30,000,000 to $40,000,000 from our sugar duties, pay a bounty to the sugar planters for a few years.

In view of the recent report of the U. S. Forestry Commission, showing the rapid cutting of our forests, and the climatic and other advantages of preserving them, the necessity of repealing the duty on lumber is especially evident, in order to save in some measure our own timber by using the stores in Canada. The duty on art works and books should be removed in the interest of education and civilization.

Such are some of the features of the present problem of revenue reduction as they appear to the writer. I regret that I cannot elaborate them more fully.

EDWARD W. BEMIS.

WAGES AND THE TARIFF.

By Professor J. Laurence Laughlin, of Harvard University.

The assertion that the tariff — that is, a *tax* on imported goods — governs the rate of wages, is made with such persistence that in the interest of sound economic teaching it deserves a candid examination. That a tax which is a subtraction from the wealth of the country should result in an addition to it, is an obvious contradiction. As generally stated, it is said that the employment of laborers depends upon the existence of the tariff; for without the tariff, it is urged, manufacturing would cease to exist, and consequently laborers would be thrown out of employment. A picture is given of the distress and misery which would follow the stoppage of great factories, now employing thousands of operatives, and it is asked where these men and women can find a place to work. The investment of capital in manufactures, they go on to say, increases the demand for laborers, and consequently wages are kept at a higher level in the United States than in England, where there is no protective tariff. Wages in the United States, moreover, are stated to have been very low at the beginning of the century, but to have risen since, because of the passage of tariff acts; and now it is claimed that if the duties were reduced the wages of American workingmen would be lowered to the level of the "pauper labor" of Europe. In looking at this matter, it will be well to see whether the glib orators who masquerade as "practical men" have taken into account all the facts of the case, or whether very important facts are constantly overlooked.

We may start out with the accepted fact that wages are generally (although not always) higher in the United States than in Europe. In no other group of industries in this country is the high rate of wages more marked than in what are known as the extractive (not solely "agricultural") industries, such as farming, stock-raising, lumbering, oil-producing, and the growing of tobacco, cotton, and hemp. From these come the products which, because of their low relative prices, are exported to foreign countries in enormous quantities. These articles head the list of our exports. The prices of our extractive industries are, in general, so low that we can sell in open competition with the whole world. But note the conclusion from this. These are the very industries in which wages are noticeably high; in other words, the very industries of the United States in which wages are admittedly highest — as in the West — are exactly those in which prices are low and which export the largest quantities of goods abroad. Here is a fact which practical men run against every day of their lives, and yet it is constantly ignored by the doctrinnaire politicians. It is not necessary to go further, and show that in a cotton mill the highest paid labor produces the goods which can be sold at the lowest price per yard. It is unnecessary to go further in illustration of the truth that high wages do not accompany high prices as cause and effect. On the contrary, efficient and well-paid labor enables the employer to sell his goods at a low price. It is not high wages, then, which prevents us from competing in foreign countries, for we already do it.

Another fact — one which is patent to every-one — is these industries which can export goods abroad get no addition to the prices of their articles by the imposition of duties on imports into the United States. In other words, our tariff cannot raise the price of wheat or corn sold to Germany.* If the duties have no effect to raise the price, then, on anything by which wages are affected by the prices of goods, wages in the extract-

*I will not here go into the discussion of international value, which is more or less abstruse. It is true that our tariff, by imposing a barrier to imports, might change the equation of international demand unfavorably to the foreigner; but this can be again equalized by retaliation on the part of the foreigner. Although, even if the foreigner did not retaliate, it is not likely that his demand for our products would remain the same, after we disturbed the equilibrium by imposing a tariff here.

ive industries are wholly unaffected by the tariff. Or on any theory by which wages are governed by the amount of capital offered to workingmen — *i.e.*, the chances for employment presented to them by men who are able to hire them—it cannot be said that wages are regulated by the tariff. It would be absurd to argue this point, if it did not offer a stumbling-block to many honest minds ; chiefly because many persons do not consider that a tariff is a tax,* a subtraction, not an addition, to the wealth or capital of a country. On no possible grounds, then, can it be said that in the extractive industries at least high wages are maintained by a protective tariff. We find a great class of our industries wholly uninfluenced by the tariff as regards the prices at which their products are sold abroad; and yet we find that wages in these industries are not only as high as (and even higher than) in manufactures, but are also very much higher than in the corresponding industries in Europe. The "pauper labor" of Europe has not ruined our farmers, nor their ability to pay high wages, and yet they send their products all over Europe. Even the seven-cent-per-day laborer of India produces no effect on the wages of our agricultural laborers. Now if the tariff cannot be the cause of high wages in the extractive industries, then the gen-

---

*It derived its name from the island of Tarifa, an island at the entrance of the Mediterranean, on which lived the robbers who exacted toll from ships going through the Straits of Gibraltar.

eral proposition that the tariff causes high wages falls to the ground; for if it does not cause high wages in some industries, why should it in others? If the tariff cannot be the cause of high wages in our extractive industries, there is no reason whatever to suppose that the tariff causes the high wages now paid in any other industries, including manufactures.

It is asserted, however, that the existence of certain protected manufactures gives a demand for labor which keeps up the level of wages to a point higher than would be the case if these manufactures ceased to exist. That is, that the level of wages in the United States is fixed by the rates paid by manufacturers, while the farmers and other employers must adopt the level fixed for them by protected manufacturers. It is claimed that the protected industries of the United States employ so much labor that their rate of wages must necessarily be paid by any other industry which hires labor. Now nothing can be further from the truth than this. It is an error based on a simple omission to consider the facts as they stand on record. The relative numbers of men and women employed in industries not affected by the tariff and those in industries affected by the tariff, is altogether misstated; and yet the facts are easy of access.

According to the census of 1880 the total number of persons engaged in gainful occupations in the United States was 17,392,099, divided as follows :—

(1) Agriculture 7,670,493
(2) Professional and Personal.... 4,074,238
(3) Trade and Transportation.... 1,810,256
(4) Manufactures, Mechanics and Mining.................... 3,837,112

Now of these persons how many are unaffected by foreign competition, and so are not recipients of any gain in the prices of their products arising from the imposition of customs duties? We may subtract* from the first class all the agricultural population of Maine, New Hampshire, Vermont, and one-half of that of New York, as possibly affected by Canadian competition, leaving 7,299,842 persons in class (1) not subject to foreign competition. Persons in the next two classes (2) and (3) are unaffected by foreign competition, because a competitor must necessarily reside in the country where the work is done or the service is rendered. So 5,884,494 more persons are not subject to foreign competition. Nor are all of class (4) affected by foreign competition. The census included in this class a large number of laborers whose industries do not feel the effect of foreign competition. To avoid cavil, I print the list herewith :—

Agricultural implements.................. 4,891
Bakers 41,309
Blacksmiths 172,726

---

*See Report of the Secretary of the Treasury, 1886, Appendix D; and Laughlin's " Mill," pp. 618-20.

Bleachers, dyers and scourers	8,222
Blind, door and sash	4,946
Boatmakers	2,063
Boot and shoemakers	194,079
Bottlers and mineral waters	2,081
Box-factory operatives	15,762
Brass founders	11,568
Brewers and malsters	16,278
Brick and tile	36,052
Bridge builders and contractors	2,587
Builders and contractors	10,804
Butchers	76,241
Cabinet-makers	50,654
Car-makers	4,708
Carpenters and joiners	373,143
Carriage and wagons	49,881
Charcoal and lime burners	5,851
Clerks and bookkeepers in manufacturing establishments	10,114
Clocks and repairing	4,354
Coopers	49,138
Distillers and rectifiers	3,245
Engineers and firemen	79,628
Fertilizers	1,383
Fishermen and oystermen	41,352
Gas works	4,695
Gilders	1,763
Gun and locksmiths	10,572
Hair-cleaners, etc	1,965
Harness and saddle makers	39,960
Jewellers	28,405
Leather, etc (not case and pocket book-makers)	29,842
Machinists	101,130
Marble and stone-cutters	32,842
Masons	102,473
Meat-preserving and packers	6,296
Millers	53,440
Milliners, dress-makers, etc	285,401
Mirror and picture-frames	2,503
Oil-mill, refinery and wells	11,269
Organ-makers	2,437
Painters and varnishers	128,556
Paper hangers	5,013
Photographers	9,990
Pianofortes	5,413
Plasterers	22,083

Plumbers and gas-fitters	19,383
Printers, etc	72,726
Pump-makers	1,366
Quarrymen	15,169
Quartz and stamp mill	1,449
Rag-pickers	2,206
Railroad builders	1,206
Roofers and slaters	4,026
Sail and awning	2,950
Sawyers	5,195
Sewing-machines	2,725
Sewing-machine operators	7,505
Shingle and lath	5,166
Shirt, collar and cuffs	11,823
Starch	1,885
Stave shook and heading	4,061
Stove, furnace and grate	3,341
Tailors	42,818
Tobacco factory	20,446
Upholsterers	10,443
Wheelwrights	15,592
Wood-choppers	12,731
Wood turners	12,954
	2,216,848

In class (4) at least 1,922,672 are not exposed to foreign competition; or in all the four classes a total of no less than 15,401,184 persons, whose wages can in no wise be said to be maintained by a tariff which shuts out foreign competition. There remain, then, only 1,990,915 laborers whose occupations can be said to be protected from foreign competition by a tariff. Moreover, in other industries included in class (4) but omitted in the above list, it is estimated that from 260,000 to 456,000 persons are not affected by foreign competition;* but it is unnecessary to include these in our estimate, in order to show

---
*Report Secretary Treasury, *ibid*.

clearly that persons engaged in the extractive and other industries, uninfluenced by foreign competition, far outnumber those affected by foreign competition. It is well within the truth to say that nine-tenths of the persons to whom wages are paid in the United States are engaged in occupations which get no protection from foreign competition. Consequently the rate of wages paid to these 15,401,184 laborers cannot be fixed or maintained by the tariff, but the rate must be due to conditions existing in this highly productive country of ours, which are wholly independent of the tariff. It cannot be said for a moment that the wages paid to 1,990,915 persons fix the rate paid to 15,401,184 persons; for it is exactly the reverse. It is never solemnly asserted that the tail wags the dog.

Another fact of great importance is also overlooked in this discussion. Wages are said to have been raised in the United States by protective tariffs, and to be kept high by the same agency; and if the tariff were reduced it is urged that wages would fall. Now how can this wholly illogical assertion be held to in the face of the fact that in free-trade England wages are higher than in protected France and Germany? And there is no dispute whatever about this fact. English laborers are much better paid, clothed, and housed, than laborers on the continent. Why does not protection in France raise wages? and why does not free trade in England lower wages? Protection in France and Germany does not begin to produce a high level of wages. Then why should it be said to do it in the United States? Does this not lead us to reflect that the high wages in our country and the low wages in Europe must be due to things other than the tariff? To claim that the tariff does one thing in the United States, and exactly the reverse in Europe, is evidently the resort of a man who will resort to any subterfuge to carry his point: he is not searching for the truth. To reason that a tariff (which is taxation) can have caused the industrial progress of the United States is to overlook the thousand things which have affected the production of wealth in this country: our wonderfully rich natural resources; the high civilization of our population from the start in a new country; the energy, intelligence, ingenuity, and power of invention of American laborers; the stimulating forces of our democratic institutions; and the enormous growth of capital, which has outstripped even the growth of population.

Moreover, those who maintain that the tariff raises wages are utterly inconsistent. They ask Congress to put on a tariff to compensate them for the high rate of American wages—to equalize the conditions of labor in Europe and America. It is an absurdity. They impale themselves on the horns of an obvious dilemma. If the tariff raises wages, then every tariff-act places (according to their way of thinking) the American employer, relatively to the foreigner, at a disadvantage due to this act. Consequently if Congress should take these people at their word, they ought to save them from higher wages by never granting tariff legislation; for they say the tariff raises wages. And then because American wages are high, they ask for protection from the foreigner! It is utterly inconsistent.

It must be evident that the high rate of wages in the United States is due to causes lying outside of the tariff. The great number of laborers employed in occupations not affected by the tariff furnish the main part of the supply of labor, and the relation of this number to capital offered for employment, together with the productiveness of our industries, fixes the general rate of wages. Moreover, these are the industries which are most productive; for, by the mere fact of needing protection, other industries give a proof that they are less productive. In B D, the more productive industries, of course, the product to be divided is larger than in A C, the less productive industries. And, if

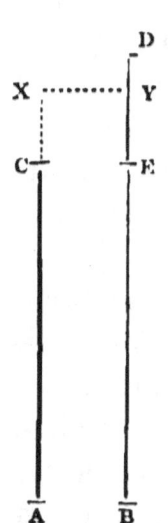

the majority of industries are like B D, the general level of wages and interest will be high. Therefore, when men want to take up industries like A C, they find that they cannot pay the same wages as in B D, and yet get as high a return for capital as is common in B D. They say that the high rate of wages prevents them from competing with foreigners, when, in reality, it is the low productiveness of their industry which, not yielding enough to pay both wages and "profits" as high as in B D, causes them to call on the state for "protection." Then, what is really done is to raise the value of the product A C to a higher level, X Y, by taking D Y from B D and giving it to A C; that is, protection takes from the more productive and adds to the less productive industries. This is done by allowing A C to sell its product at a price as high as that of the foreign goods, plus the duty; or the price of goods in A C is raised relatively to those in B D, which means that the goods of A C exchange for more of the goods of B D; or, *vice versa*, that more of the goods of B D are given for the goods of A C than before; so that a part of B D goes to A C because of the tariff. Then, with this addition taken from B D, A C is able to pay the same wages and interest as B D, while B D must pay less in wages and interest than without protection.

Instead of laborers being protected by the tariff, it is claimed that by the tariff the articles of common use, such as coats, hats, blankets, woollen goods, and shoes, are increased in price by the tariff, and the workingman must pay this increased price just because the manufacturer does not want to change his business. If the duties on wool and woollen goods were abolished, every man could get his clothing at about one-half the present price. Without protection, not only would wages be larger, but the articles he buys would be cheaper.

J. Laurence Laughlin.

THE SCIENTIFIC BASIS OF TARIFF LEGISLATION.*

By Hon. Carroll D. Wright, United States Commissioner of Labor.

In a commercial sense there are two great parties in this country, the free traders and the protectionists. The two great political parties have not, in recent years, drawn their lines distinctively on the issue of free trade and protection, because the two great commercial parties furnish a large portion of the members of the two great political parties, and so interchangeable and so thoroughly interwoven are the commercial elements with the political elements, that such a division is not likely to occur until one or the other system of commerce, or of

---

*Note.—Col. Wright was requested to furnish for this collection a paper discussing the bearings of the protective system upon the condition of American workingmen and the extent to which this consideration should have weight in the revision of our revenue system. He replied that there was not, to his mind, a line of facts in existence which would enable one intelligently to discuss that question. Furthermore, he was, very properly, not willing to say anything publicly relating to the tariff which would seem in any way to anticipate conclusions that might be deducible from the Labor Bureau's future investigation of the cost of production or that might be in any quarter prejudicial to the report on that subject. In lieu, therefore, of the paper asked for, Col. Wright gave permission to use an address made by him a few years ago on the scientific basis of tariff legislation. It is so thoroughly pertinent to the current discussion that it is reprinted here in full. The address was originally read before the American Social Science Association, at Saratoga, September 10, 1884.—[Edr.]

trade, can be demonstrated beyond a doubt as the best system or policy for this country to adopt. This condition exists because the discussion of the tariff is still carried on within the realms of theory, neither party being able to demonstrate the correctness of its theory when reduced to practice. Of course, all true theories must be true in practice in the long run, but the difficulty is that some conditions essential to the perfect working out of the theory do not exist when the principles of the theory come to be applied. This is very clearly illustrated in one of the great fundamental features of the tariff discussion.

There are in this country 90,000 operatives engaged in the manufacture of woollens; it is true, theoretically, that if woollen goods can be manufactured cheaper by English, French, German, or other operatives, than by the American, the American consumer is entitled to the benefit of such cheaper manufacture, and that the 90,000 woollen operatives should therefore vacate their trade, and seek some other occupation, and let the manufacture of woollens take place where it can be done on the cheapest basis. This, theoretically, is the true doctrine without doubt, but, in order to have it work practically, we must, in the first place, secure the perfect mobility of labor, and until such mobility can be secured, the theory, however fine, or however true, cannot find a practical application, because, as the conditions of industry now exist, such a number of operatives could not successfully seek other employment. This immobility of labor does not antagonize the theory at all, even in practice, for, theoretically, the 90,000 woollen operatives would, in the long run, either find something else to do, or live a miserable existence until they needed nothing more to do. So, the theories of the free trader and of the protectionist, as illustrated by this one instance, cannot be so clearly demonstrated to the common mind as to make the tariff question as yet a clearly defined political issue.

The discussion is still further involved, and, to a great extent, by the want of illustration, that is, of sufficient data, whereby either theory can be clearly demonstrated; the advocates of the two great systems depend so largely upon assertion and assumption, and so little upon actual facts, that the common verdict, reached by the majority of the people, is that the tariff is a muddle, and even enlightened men, who have not made a special study of the question, do not hesitate to say that they do not understand what it means.

The advocates of each great commercial system bring to their advocacy great learning and great intelligence, and, we are bound to say when we look at the character of the advocates, thorough integrity; and we must also assume that each party, as represented by its members, is seeking only the good of the whole country; and yet sometimes, the asperity of the discussion, and it is too often so, would indicate that each thinks the other party is seeking only the destruction of the industries of the nation. Honest men honestly believe in the correctness of the positions they assume with reference to this great question, for this question is either a vital one, or it is not; the tariff either has a great influence on the prosperity of the masses of a country, or it has not; the welfare and the happiness of the wage receivers are enhanced by the existing policy, or they are not; the industries of a country are either built up, or restricted in their building up, by the influence of tariff legislation; the people are robbed, or they are not robbed, through import duties; they are swindled as consumers, or they are not, through the influence of these duties; and taking these questions as fundamental in the tariff discussion the tariff question does become a vital one, and if it is a vital question now, it has been a vital question in the past, and must be so until it is settled; and yet with these vital elements there are two sides, each of which is hotly fought. And this hot contest, it would seem to an ordinary observer, should have been productive of sufficient intelligent data, on which legislation could be correctly based, long ere this.

A very brief and casual study of tariff legislation in the United States, proves to any one that it has not been carried through on any clearly defined basis, or on a sufficiently clearly defined basis to admit of saying that the tariffs of the past have been constructed on scientific groundwork.

It is not my purpose in this paper to discuss the merits or the demerits of either of the great commercial systems. With the exception of England, the protective principle is adopted in nearly all great producing countries, I mean those countries which are engaged in manufactures. In the United States, the free trade party finds its warmest adherents among the economists, students, and those generally who seek the practical application of theoretical systems, and among the great importers. On the other hand, the protectionist party finds its most active adherents among the producers themselves, including the manufacturers and the people they employ, and the producers of raw materials. Here then we have two well defined parties, the theorists on the one side, and the business men, or those who must apply principles practically, on the other side. The merits and the demerits of the two great systems are so often and so forcibly set forth by the respective advocates, that no necessity exists for their discussion at the present time. So far as the motive of this paper is concerned then, the rights and the wrongs of the question are not to be considered, but taking the system which exists as one likely to exist for some years at least, the first duty we have in the premises, it seems to me, is, to make our legislation depend upon clearly defined bases, and not upon haphazard statements, and not upon the representations of self interest alone

I presume it is perfectly true that when the tariff acts of the past have been constructed, manufacturers made such representations to the proper congressional committee as in their judgment would indicate for the industries involved the true basis for the establishment of rates. But they could have only the crudest facts on which to base such a judgment; the best part of it was their knowledge of the markets of the world, and of the cost of manufacture, as obtained from very crude data, and the cost of importation, that is, of freight, but they had no well established data on which to make their recommendations to Congress, and so our tariff acts represent a wide range of judgment, resulting in a wide range of rates of duty, any attempt to readjust which, has only resulted in more and greater discrepancies in the range.

My purpose then, is to show:

1st. What I mean by a scientific basis for tariff legislation.

2nd. The necessity for such basis.

3rd. How can such a basis be secured?

And 4th. What would be the results of legislation based upon such a basis?

The *First* point, what is a scientific basis, is very briefly answered.

The basis which shall enable legislation to be clearly defined, and just in its operation in every particular, if any legislation is to be had at all, may properly be called a scientific basis.

When facts can be classified in such a way as to show their truth, which truth can be uniformly applied, you have reduced the matter to a science, which is, to quote Worcester, "the knowledge of many methodically digested and arranged so as to become attainable by one." It is knowledge certain and evident in itself. A classification of the facts which bear upon a tariff and by which certain absolute positions as to rates become established, would constitute a scientific basis, as the term is used in this paper, and such classification should be the result of such a wide collection of individual facts as to leave no doubt in the mind of any man, whether free trader or protectionist, of the position to be attained relative to each great industry. I am, however, well aware that such a basis, even when reached, would be to some extent a temporary one, but I am also convinced that the temporary features of such a basis would relate only to degree and not to the fundamental value of the basis itself, that is to say, the changes in industrial conditions are as a rule so slight, that the variation in the basis scientifically reached would not invalidate its usefulness to any great extent for just legislation. Great industrial disasters, from whatever cause, might result in the radical disturbance of some of the compositions determined by a scientific classification of data, but were such the case, the same methods which secured the original basis would secure its scientific readjustment, so that the criticism which might perhaps properly be made upon the basis which I shall indicate, has not deterred me from prosecuting my study.

Second. Is there any necessity for a basis such as that indicated? To my own mind there is, and I come to this conclusion from the character of the discussion between the two great commercial parties, and from my own observations extending over a number of years.

A recital of some of the leading points made by the advocates of each great system would indicate the necessity of some basis even for discussion, whether we have a basis for legislation or not. One following the discussions will notice that American free traders allege that protection is the cause of the frequent recurrence of labor difficulties in this country, while English free traders allege that our protective policy causes English labor difficulties. Again, English manufacturers have in many instances said to me, when asking the cause of the silent looms and machines in their works, that they are rendered silent by our protective policy; at the same time, in argument, they have always claimed that the application of their national policy in America would secure a far greater industrial prosperity in this country than has yet been witnessed. Again, it is claimed by the advocates of free trade that the wonderful industrial prosperity which has blessed the English people is due entirely to their policy of free trade, while all protectionists claim that the wonderful industrial prosperity which has blessed the people of the United States is due entirely to protection.

Two or three illustrations of these adverse claims may be necessary.

John Bright, who certainly is an ardent free trader, in his well known speech at Birmingham in June, 1883, on the presentation to him of an address and plate, at the Bright celebration, made a very careful review of the industrial condition of England now, as compared with what it was before the adoption of free trade. He showed by facts and figures which cannot be disputed, that wages were higher, that the condition of the workingman is better, and that the progress of the country during the period stated had been wonderful indeed, all of which, he claimed, was due to the adoption of the principle of free trade. If you should turn from Mr. Bright's speech to the multitude of speeches in favor of protection made in the United States Congress during the last session, during the debate on the Morrison bill, or in speeches made whenever the subject of the tariff has been before Congress, or if you will refer to any of the protectionist writers, or if you want something more easily reached, Mr. Blaine's letter of acceptance, you will find it claimed without exception that American prosperity is due to the protective policy of our government. One can pick up any of the pamphlets which are issued in advocacy of either of the two great principles, and find plenty of evidence of the truth of the statement I have made. Both these claims cannot be correct.

Again, it is alleged that the periodical stagnation or depression in American industrial enterprises is largely, if not wholly, due to protection, because protection prevents our manufacturers from finding a foreign market for their surplus goods, and that free trade here would prevent such recurrence, while the fact exists that in Great Britain, under free trade, the same conditions are met with, and that stagnation there when it does come, is as severe as any that we experience. The American and the English manufacturer alike demand extended markets for their surplus.

There is something in this besides the influence of free trade and protection

The free trader, urging the adoption of free trade in America in order that surplus products may be sold abroad, claims at the same time that "there are scores of profitable industries that cannot now be carried on in this country on account of the tariff, but would spring into existence as soon as it was removed."* On the other hand, the equally intelligent protectionist says in substance, there are scores of industries now carried on because the tariff does exist, that with its removal would be abandoned.

Which of these two propositions can be demonstrated as true? One must be false, but it is said by a prominent writer that the guarantee for the anticipation of the results of the adoption of the English system "is in a correct understanding of the laws of production and commerce."† Such an understanding would also settle the question relative to the extension of trade, so as to secure a market for the surplus products of both free trade and protective countries. I am afraid that the conditions of Prof. Sumner's guarantee cannot be accepted for

---

*W. G. Sumner, in "North American Review," September. 1884.
†Ibid.

many generations. Certainly not while eminent doctors disagree.

Again, it is claimed by ardent protectionists that protection is the sole cause, or if they do not go so far, that it is the leading cause, of the advance of wages in America, while the free trader, on the other hand, claims that the advance of wages in Great Britain is due to the policy of free trade, while any careful investigation will show that there has been an advance in wages during the last fifty years in both countries, and that so far as the manufacture of textiles is concerned the advance has been nearly equal under the two great commercial systems.* This one fact shows that the claims of each party as to wages is entirely without foundation

The discoverer of the causes which regulate the rates of wages has not yet seen fit to give his name to the public. It is perfectly easy to discuss the question of wages in various lights, and to assume this, that, or the other cause as most powerful in their regulation, and yet one rises from a study of such discussions entirely unsatisfied.

My friend, Mr. Atkinson, has come nearer to a satisfactory explanation than any other writer, or rather, I should say, nearer to the practical demonstration of the best theory on the subject than any other writer. Probably President

---

*See chapter on Wages in "Factory System," Vol. 2, Report on the United States Census for 1880

Walker has more clearly stated a theory which can be demonstrated than any of his contemporaries; but the great causes are still beyond such demonstration as will satisfy all men alike of their fundamental character. Certainly, the permanent influence of the tariff upon wages is a mooted question.

To be sure, the protectionist quotes the high wages of America to substantiate his ground, and he puts them in comparison with the lower wages of England; the free trader turns upon the protectionist, and while he admits the higher wages of America quotes the low wages of the protectionist countries of Europe in comparison with the rates paid in the free trade country of England. I have been waiting to see some writer go still further in the race, and quote the still lower wages of countries way down in the scale of civilization in comparison with the rates paid in the protective countries of Europe.

The free trader, without being able even to hint at the proof of his assertion, knocks the protectionist down with the statement that wages are high in America notwithstanding the tariff, and would be whether we had a tariff or not. The protectionist trips up the heels of the free trader by his assumption that wages are higher in England than on the continent without regard to the tariff, and thus each uses the other's arguments so far as wages are concerned to prove himself in a muddle, and we get no nearer the truth, and the whole discussion consists largely of assertions and assumptions.

Again, it is observed that nearly all the arguments in favor of either great system of commerce are usually based upon the same array of statistics, when statistics are used, and the student who does not care which system prevails but who is simply seeking the true one, concludes that, as a rule, the pretended arguments are mere assumptions, the assumptions being the results of the theory of the speaker or writer, and that the theory is usually the result of his relation to the industries of the country. That my own statement in this respect may not mark my own condemnation, and be considered a mere assumption, allow me to illustrate:

In a little work entitled " Wages, Living, and Tariff," by Mr. E. A. Hartshorn, now prominently before the public, the results in the United States of the various tariff measures, or rather the results of the two systems of commerce during a period of seventy years from 1813 to 1883, have been summarized, and from this summary we find that the writer concludes that under the free trade or revenue tariffs, as established in 1817, 1834, 1846, and 1857, labor was seeking employment, wages low, emigration declining, farm products low, manufactures high, revenue, public and private, small and decreasing, bankruptcy nearly universal, the national status one of growing dependence, and the national credit bad; while under the protective tariffs, as established in 1813, 1828, 1842, and 1861, labor was in demand, wages high, manufactured products low, public and private revenues large and increasing, public and private wealth increasing, the national status one of growing independence, and the national credit good; and the writer then remarks, "In the presence of these important historical facts, let the candid reader remember that the American people have never yet attained the best results of protection, nor the worst results of free trade," and further he asks this question, "If the results of partial protection to labor have been so satisfactory, and the results of partial free trade so unsatisfactory, which system shall we choose?"

In laying down Mr. Hartshorn's pamphlet, and picking up the admirable treatise of Mr. Henry Loomis Nelson, entitled, "Our Unjust Tariff Law," we find in his chapter on "What a low tariff did for the country," the following statement:—"There never was a period of greater prosperity in the history of the country," and then he goes on with an elaborate and very carefully adjusted statement of facts to prove the correctness of his assertion, and concludes, while referring to the very tariffs which Mr. Hartshorn claimed were productive of so much evil, by saying, "No other decade, except that during which the country was blessed with a revenue tariff, has such a story of prosperity to tell as these ten years have stamped on our history. No other decade will have such a story to tell, until the government ceases to tax four-fifths of the people for the benefit of a small fraction of the other fifth."

I have quoted these two little works to illustrate my point, instead of quoting larger and more elaborate treatises, and perhaps more standard works, because these two that I have named are prepared with apparent candor and integrity, and are being widely read at the present time by the people; but the same features might be illustrated, and very fully too, from older and more standard works. Certainly if we turn to the newspapers of the day, we find statistics relative to imports and exports, and the trade and productions of the country, brought into elaborate tables, and arrayed on either side, and if we did not know the tendency of the paper in which we found these arrays of figures, we should not know upon which side they were used as arguments, unless the writer was careful to announce his point.

The feat is constantly attempted of bringing diverse conclusions from the same premises. A recent writer*quotes the low interest at present paid for the use of capital in this country, as a demonstration that obstruction to imports or exports immediately acts to reduce the value of capital; but what has reduced the rate of interest in England? Our own rates of interest are now approaching the rates of interest paid in Great Britain. What has the tariff to do with it?

The same writer, with all the facts before him, concludes that the average rate of wages paid in American cotton mills, in proportion to the number of hours at work, is actually less than it is in England; and then, after arraigning the theories of his opponents, says, that "all these theories are the purest assumptions, not warranted by facts, and directly contrary to experience and reason." This is exactly the charge made by protectionists, and upon the same array of facts.

Another charge which is reciprocally made is, that "men whose minds have once closed with a good grip on a dogma, never give it up on account of facts of experience, or on account of absurdities into which it carries them."

All these attempts to secure antagonistic conclusions from a single premise, thoroughly illustrate the necessity of a scientific basis, not only for tariff legislation, but for tariff discussion.

With the one secured, the other follows. This

---
*Thos. G. Shearman, "North American Review," September, 1884.

necessity is further illustrated by a study of the rates of duty established by law, and when this study is made, it is no wonder that the tariff is declared to be a muddle. The table showing the excess of tariff duties over cost of labor, prepared by Hon. Thomas J. Wood, of Indiana, for use in debate on the Morrison tariff bill, is exceedingly valuable in this connection. By this table it is shown that the smallest excess under the existing tariff is 5 per cent., and the largest about 80 per cent. A comparison of the wage statistics reported in the Fifteenth Annual Report of the Massachusetts Bureau of Statistics of Labor, where the percentage of excess of wages paid in Massachusetts over those paid in Great Britain* in like industries is mathematically

---

*The disparity between the average wages paid in certain industries in Great Britain and Massachusetts, and the average duty laid on the products of such industries, is shown in the following table:

INDUSTRIES.	Average weekly wages higher in Massachusetts than in Great Britain by percentages, as follows:	Average duty laid under existing laws Per cent.
Agricultural Implements,	15.8	35 to 40
Artisans' Tools,	141.3	45
Boots and Shoes,	166.1	30
Brick	107.5	20
Carpetings,	47.9	49.78
Carriages and Wagons,	182.2	35
Clothing	49.1	35 to 60
Cotton Goods	88.4	38.3
Food Preparations	260.7	20
Furniture	38.7	35
Glass	76.9	25.2 to 68.5
Hats	99.8	35 to 50
Hosiery	39.0	40 to 55
Metals and Metallic Goods	52.0	45
Printing and Publishing	106.0	25
Wooden Goods	115.0	85
Woollen Goods	42.0	64
Worsted Goods	103.3	49.8

stated, with the rates of duties affecting the same industries, would show a discrepancy as large as that displayed by the table prepared by Mr. Wood.

These two statistical illustrations show most forcibly the necessity of a scientific basis, so far as arguments drawn from like premises are concerned.

Again, one party asserts that the people are robbed through the action of the tariff, that the manufacturer may gain wealth; while the other side as strenuously asserts that the manufacturer gains nothing beyond his legitimate due, and that the payment of taxes for the support of the national government through consumption is the easiest method for providing for our national budget. One of these propositions must be false, and the proper basis for tariff legislation would prove which one is false.

Finally, the necessity of such a basis as I have indicated is proved, because no adequate data exists for determining the indicative points presented.

Third. If there is a necessity for a scientific basis for tariff legislation, how can it be reached?

Such a basis can be reached only through a knowledge of all the facts bearing upon the question, and these facts have not as yet been classified. They may have been collected in part and exist in fugitive condition, but as yet without thorough classification. To reach this classification, I submit four propositions:

PROPOSITION I. *a.* There should be a classification of all articles on which a duty is now laid, and the rates on each article.

b. There should be a classification of articles on which duties are now laid, showing those articles the duties on which are intended for protection, and those on which the duties are laid simply for securing revenue.

c. A classification of such articles as are produced in this and other countries, and in what countries.

d. A classification of such articles as are produced in other countries only, and in what countries.

e. A classification of duties imposed upon such articles under the various tariffs.

f. A classification of what may be termed natural industries of the various countries in competition with the United States.

PROPOSITION II. *a.* A collection and classification of data relating to the composition of the product of all leading articles named in Proposition I, and showing the percentage of labor, raw material, etc., entering into the product in each of the leading countries where such articles are produced, such data to be collected entirely from original sources.

b. The collection and classification of data, showing the cost, including all elements up to the selling price of such articles in the leading countries where they are produced, such data to be collected on samples as far as possible.

c. A list of jobbing and retail prices of all such articles in the countries where produced.

d. The cost of importation of such articles as are produced in countries abroad.

e. A list of jobbing and retail prices in this country of such articles.

f. The jobbing and retail prices of like articles produced in this country.

g. A summary of prices of such articles with and without duty charges, and under various tariffs so far as possible.

[This proposition involves rates of wages paid, in the industries involved, in various countries, the efficiency of labor in the countries involved, the capacity of machinery and all other elements affecting cost of production; and the mathematical working out of the results of the proposition would show exactly what consumers of articles imported and produced here pay for goods on account of the tariff, and what they would have to pay if no duty were laid on the articles named. It would also enable one to find that rate of duty absolutely essential to place the

American producer on an equal footing, and on the same footing, so far as goods offered for sale in our markets are concerned, with the foreign producer, the foreign producer having thereby no advantage in this country that he would not have were his works located here. With such a rate in our leading industries, which would be a mathematically correct rate, duties could be levied on that rate, or above it, or below it, as the exigencies of the country might demand, but the people would know the exact point, and that a duty laid above it would be for protection as well as for revenue. If the rate were laid exactly on the rate mathematically determined, then the consumer would know that he was paying the same for his goods that he would pay were there no foreign manufacturers of the same goods in existence. If a duty above this mathematical point were laid, the consumer would know that he was paying something toward the running expenses of the government, and that at the same time he was aiding in the exclusion of foreign products.

[The working out of this Proposition II, would also enable the United States Government to adopt, with regard to every leading industry, the well established principle adopted by the British Government, and as at present practiced by that Government, of laying a duty on the importation of certain articles on which an excise tax is laid at home, so that the importer shall have no advantage over the home manufacturer on account of the excise tax paid by the latter.]

PROPOSITION III. *a.* A classification of data, showing the amount of tax paid by consumers on account of tariff, such amount to be shown by means of budgets of annual expenses of families in various grades of life.

b. Data showing what a "per capita" tax would be on the basis of our national expenses, should the revenue be raised by such a tax.

c. Data showing what a property tax would be on the basis of raising our national revenue by such a tax.

d. Comparative statistics giving the results of the data as to the three methods, namely, per capita, property, and an import duty method of raising our public revenue.

[The working out of this proposition would show which method would bear the lightest and the most justly on the people, and it would also show what grade of consumers, using the word grade with relation to annual expenses, bears the tax burden chiefly.]

PROPOSITION IV. A statement of the preceding propositions, mathematically wrought out.

These propositions embody only the leading features of what I should call a basis for securing the proper information for ascertaining a rate of duty in each industry which should equalize the advantages and disadvantages of foreign and domestic producers, and the process of taxation by which the consumer should be justly taxed, and by which he should know whether he was being justly taxed or not

If a single illustration of the point I would attain, with regard to each leading industry, is required, it will be found in the supposition, that if in woollen goods, after the collection and analysis of the information I have indicated, and all other information relative thereto, it should be found that the American producer of broadcloth stands at a disadvantage of $1.00 per yard as compared with the British producer of the same kind of goods, then a tax of $1.00 per yard would simply place the foreign and American producer on an equality; in other words, the American manufacturer of broadcloths, if a tax of $1.00 per yard were laid on his product, would have no inducement to abandon his factory in America and set it up in England. If the tax of $1.00 per yard were not laid, it would be for his interest to abandon his factory in America, and move to England, or to Canada, or out of the country somewhere, where the same conditions which give the foreign producer the advantage of $1.00 per yard exist, and there set up his works. Having a tax, exactly and mathe matically determined, as essential to place the foreign and domestic manufacturers on an equality, the consumer of broadcloth is simply aiding in preserving that equality when he purchases broadcloth, and through the duty which he pays, he is not enabling the manufacturer to ask any more for his yard of broadcloth than he would if no duty were laid. The revenue is preserved and no advantage given to the American producer, nor is he placed at a disadvantage through the location of his factories in this country instead of in some other. If now Congress wished to protect the American manufacturer of broadcloth, that is to say, put him in a position where the foreign producer of the same goods could not compete with him, then any tax or rate of duty on broadcloth above $1.00 per yard would be essential, and he could ask a higher price for his goods on that account, and the home consumer could purchase the foreign article if he chose, although it would be enhanced in price on account of the duty beyond the one dollar. The distance beyond the $1.00 per yard of the duty laid upon broadcloth would determine whether the duty was a protective one or a revenue duty only, and the public would know exactly what kind of duty it was paying.

The result of this illustration, if it could be applied to all leading articles, would soon define the lines of the parties in this country, and would soon determine the question of how far a tariff shall become protective. Do not misunderstand me in the use of the word protective. I use it in its literal sense, that the protective duty excludes foreign products. The consumers, under the basis I have indicated, would clearly understand the question.

One of the chief advantages of determining mathematically the rates essential in each great industry to the preservation of equality between the domestic and foreign producer, would be in the wise adjustment, or, rather, extension of the free list ; that is to say, with the results of such a basis we would know exactly what articles could be placed upon the free list without injury to the domestic producer.

The great question of the reduction of the surplus revenue, which now disturbs the minds of the people, would be easily settled, or at least the surplus could be so adjusted that it would not be a source of anxiety to those who see in the accumulation of surplus a danger far exceeding that attending a great indebtedness.

One of the chief results, and to my own mind the most just result, of legislation upon such a basis as I have outlined, lies in the fact that all articles would be taxed with perfect fairness and equality. I cannot better illustrate this than by quoting from J. B. Sargent's recent article on the "Evils of the Tariff System," found in the September "North American Review": "No article is entitled to a higher tariff for protection than any other; or, in other words, the people should not be compelled by the Government to pay to the producer of any one article a greater percentage of extortion than is paid on another. In all cases where one article has a higher rate of tariff than another, either no attempt to produce the higher rate article should ever have been attempted in this country, or there was improper and unholy scheming by, and favoritism to, the producers or manufacturers of it."

The morality of this proposition cannot be controverted.

A further advantage of correctly adjusted duties lies in the ease with which they are readjusted. Under the conditions indicated, a bill for the horizontal readjustment of rates would be logical.

I am perfectly well aware that, as regards some industries, the attempt has been made, on a limited scale, to apply the force of the facts especially to the correct adjustment of tariff rates. This has been notably so in this country in the woollen industry; but even here the application has been only one of degree.

I am also aware that the carrying out of the propositions laid down would involve on the part of Congress quite a large appropriation. I believe all the data indicated could be collected, classified, and each rate mathematically wrought out, at an expense not exceeding $50,000; but the expense, even at $100,000, would be productive of far greater good than has been secured by much larger appropriations for similar purposes, but without similar motives.

I cannot, of course, say where an investigation of the nature indicated would lead politically, whether it would aid the party of free traders or the party of protectionists; but I am of the opinion that it would lead to a discovery of rates which would be mathematically and scientifically correct, and morally just to all. The working out of the propositions laid down must be done fearlessly and without regard to results, for the necessary investigations should be made with a patriotic view of benefiting the consumers and the producers, without reference to individual interests.

I am sure there is nothing chimerical in the scheme; on the other hand, I am sure, from the necessities of the case, that with such a basis as I have indicated, or any other which will secure the results which I think this would secure, the tariff question would assume a simplicity in its constituent elements which would enable all men to understand it, and which would secure its early and final removal from the politics of the country. Certainly these are results to be desired by all patriotic citizens.

CARROLL D. WRIGHT.

CONCLUSION.

By the Editor.

It is not the purpose of the editor to attempt a complete summary or review of the opinions expressed in the foregoing essays. Each reader may well be left to sum up for himself. Yet, without any desire to make authoritative interpretation, there may be noted a few general conclusions that seem to be justified.

1. The contributors to this volume are all in favor of some revision of the revenue system of the United States Government. All are in favor of changes which, in their opinion, will tend to lessen and to equalize the burdens of taxation. All, or practically all, are in favor of changes that will result in a material reduction of ordinary revenue.

2. It is vigorously urged by several contributors,—notably Professors Adams and Seligman, and President Walker—that a federal government like ours cannot, without grave evils and constant danger, have a volume of ordinary revenue considerably larger than the volume of ordinary expenditure. Professor Wilson also especially urges the importance of a close relation between income and expenditure, and the periodical readjustment of the former to the requirements of the latter. It would perhaps be fair to

conclude that all, or nearly all, of the contributors to these pages hold that the Government's annual receipts should be limited as strictly as possible to an amount equal to the sum total of such annual expenditures, for all purposes, as Congress deliberately decides to be wise and necessary. This view places expenditure first and taxation second.

3. It would also, however, seem to be generally agreed that, while revenue should be adjusted carefully and periodically to meet wise demands for expenditure, the reduction should be made in such a way as not to cripple the financial resources of the Government. Thus, Professor Adams urges that in time of peace various sources of income should be kept below the maximum revenue-yielding point. And others hold it to be a maxim that the Government should keep several strings attached to its bow, for ready use in time of need.

4. President Walker regards the surplus revenue as a subject for distinct treatment. He holds that this immediate problem should be solved without reference to the permanent policy of the Government as regards the main features of a revenue system. He thinks that all parties should be able to agree in a day upon a bill reducing revenue,—a bill so framed as not to disturb the *status quo* of contending parties on tariff or internal revenue questions. Professor

Thompson's suggestions are in the same line. Professors Ely, Adams, Smith, and others, also seem to hold that the surplus situation should not be taken advantage of for the purpose of forcing a fight against protection. Probably it would be just to infer that American economists would agree with President Walker, that the surplus should be dealt with immediately, and in such a way as not to prejudice other and more permanent issues.

As the best way to restore to circulation the large sum of "net cash" that has accumulated in the Treasury since the summer of 1887, Professor Thompson urges distribution among the States. Professor Adams discusses the plan of distribution, and opposes it; but what he really argues against is the maintenance of a superabundant revenue, and the regular practice of distribution. After the adoption of a bill pruning down the federal income to a correspondence with expenditures, he would perhaps not strenuously object to the distribution of the amount on hand. He does not regard the purchase of bonds in open market as economical. Professor Ely urges the adoption by Congress of a policy of large expenditure for public improvements of productive value to the country, especially waterway improvements. Some contributors favor a plan of refunding, and the application of the accumulated surplus to debt reduction.

There is perhaps only one general conclusion to be drawn from the various expressions on this subject of the use to be made of the accumulated money, and that is this: The presence of money in the Treasury is not a valid argument for any kind of expenditure; and no project ought to be entered upon, the wisdom of which could be doubtful if taxes had to be levied especially to meet its expense. This maxim might not have the assent of all, but a majority would probably agree with Professor Hadley in accepting it.

6. As to the sources of national revenue, the contributors for the most part use the historical mode of approaching the question. They find the federal government obtaining its income from indirect taxation. They accept this as a settled fact. Historically, the principal source of revenue has been customs duties upon imported goods. It is easily within bounds to say that American economists agree that customs duties must remain, at least for an indefinite period, the principal source of ordinary revenue. Several contributors would regard a national tax on private incomes as a desirable source of revenue; but none urge it as now feasible.

7. The proposition that the internal revenue system be abolished does not meet with acceptance. Its retention is favored by every contrib-

utor. Professor Richmond Smith makes a conclusive argument on this subject. He shows that the Government should not rely upon a single source of income, customs duties being constantly variable in amount and certain to yield least when large revenue is most needed. Whiskey and tobacco are regarded by economists as proper and desirable articles upon which to levy taxes. If abandoned by the federal Government as articles of taxation, they would probably be subjected to heavy revenue charges by the States. It might have been shown by Professor Smith, in addition to his other arguments, that a federal tax on spirits and tobacco is much more equal in its operation than a tax levied by the States would be. The consumers ultimately pay the tax, and the consumers are pretty evenly distributed throughout the Union. But the great bulk of the tobacco and spirits is produced in a few States, as is shown by the reports of the Commissioner of Internal Revenue. Thus the States of Illinois, Kentucky, etc., would be enabled to levy heavily for their public treasuries upon consumers in all parts of the Union, the tax being collected at the point of production. Evidently it is more just to all that revenues from these articles be paid to the general Government.

8. Professor Folwell distinguishes the tariff question as one of National economy rather than

one of general political economy, and discusses it from that point of view. This useful distinction, it may fairly be said, is in effect observed by most of the contributors to the volume. Ours is an age of nations and nation-building. In an infinite number of ways the State touches the social and industrial life of its citizens. Whether, in the promotion of the independence and the symmetrical growth of the nation's industries, protective tariffs are wise and beneficial, is to be studied as a question of fact in the light of all the circumstances. American economists no longer attempt to overthrow protection with a dogma, a syllogism, or a universal maxim. As Professor Seligman says: "The sway of the Manchester school is gone." Economists are not precisely agreed as to the extent to which America should henceforth maintain a protective policy; but all are united in holding that these practical problems of statesmanship are not to be settled upon any mere statement of *a priori* considerations, but rather upon painstaking and impartial study of the facts, with the aid of science and in the spirit of patriotism. So far as modern economists are concerned, the old division between Free Traders and Protectionists is disappearing rapidly. Questions at issue are those of practical policy rather than those of theory.

9. The chief difficulty about the practical readjustment of the tariff is seen to lie in the fact

that it exists at once for revenue and for the encouragement of home production. Protective considerations aside, it would be a comparatively easy task to adjust the tariff for revenue purposes. But to combine the two objects intelligently and advantageously is not an easy task. This difficulty evidently leads some economists who accept Protection as a theory, to doubt the practical expediency of maintaining it on a very extensive scale. The general verdict seems to be in favor of simplification. Yet the practical unanimity with which the contributors seem to favor the placing on the free list of all articles wholly or chiefly produced abroad and not susceptible of large production at home, would show that in their opinion the protective idea should be present, at least incidentally, in the future arrangements of our tariff schedules. Thus, there seems to be something like accord in favor of placing sugar on the free list with tea and coffee, or at least in favor of a large reduction of the duty on unrefined sugar.

10. There seems, also, something like a common opinion to the effect that the next step in tariff readjustment should be in the line of free, or freer, crude articles and materials used in manufactures. If the editor may be pardoned a a suggestion of his own, it would seem that the economists have yet more carefully to analyse these so-called "raw materials," and to distin-

guish between those that are the crude product of the forest and the mine and those that are the result of a diversified agriculture. To differentiate and intensify agriculture may be as proper an object of the protective policy as to build up manufactures.

11. President Walker's interesting analysis, which seems to have the indorsement of Professors Canfield, Ely, and others, places the burden of protective tariffs upon the agricultural interest. This analysis is exceedingly valuable, and would seem to be impregnable as far as it goes. But the editor may again be pardoned for suggesting a further step in the analysis. President Walker's distinction between those primary trades and industries that are immediately adjunct to an agricultural community and those which may be located abroad because their products are transportable, is clear and useful ; but agriculture should itself also be similarly analyzed. The farming industries of a non-manufacturing country become wholly transformed when manufactures are established.

Simple wheat-raising—the lowest form of agriculture—gives place to stock growing, dairying, fruit culture, gardening, and in general the production of articles which are demanded by the home market, but could not be sent to foreign markets. This diversified agriculture is vastly more profitable than the raising of cereals, and it quadruples the value of farming lands. Does not this change in the character of agriculture quite compensate the farmer, or even more than compensate him, for the higher price he has to pay at the outset for the articles of manufacture produced in his neighborhood under a protective policy? It is not here asserted that this is the case; but the query is made by way of suggestion. The hard conditions of agriculture which Professor Canfield describes as existing in Kansas are those of cereal raising in a new region. They do not exist in the older States, from the Atlantic coast to the Mississippi river, where primary agriculture has given way to a large diversification of farming on account of the local markets furnished by the up-building of non-agricultural industries. Is it not quite possible that, if American manufactures had not been encouraged under the protective policy, Ohio, Indiana and Illinois would now be producing our export wheat, while Kansas, Nebraska and Dakota lands would not as yet have been called into requisition? The editor has no wish to controvert the views of his contributors, and only adds these hints by way of extending, possibly, the field of the inquiry.

12. Commissioner Wright's admirable outline of a statistical and scientific basis for tariff legislation would doubtless have the indorsement of a great majority of American economists. In

the same line is Professor Ely's proposal for an expert and impartial tariff commission. It is perceived that the current discussions turn chiefly upon questions of fact, and that modern statistical science can be trusted to answer many of those questions with approximate accuracy.

ALBERT SHAW.

APPENDIX

OF

STATISTICAL TABLES.

ANALYSIS OF UNITED STATES REVENUES FOR THE YEAR ENDING JUNE 30, 1887.

From Customs	$217,286,893.13
From Internal Revenue	118,823,391.22
From Sales of Public Lands	9,254,286.42
From Profits on Coinage, Bullion Deposits and Assays	8,929,252.83
From Tax on National Banks	2,395,851.18
From Fees—Consular, Letters Patent, and Land	3,301,647.16
From Customs Fees, Fines, Penalties, etc.	1,053,037.86
From Sales of Indian Lands	1,479,028.81
From Soldiers' Home, Permanent Fund	1,226,239.47
From Sinking-Fund for Pacific Railways	1,364,435.87
From Repayment of Interest by Pacific Railways	914,793.13
From Sales of Old Public Buildings	624,882.20
From Sales of Government Property	262,832.32
From Immigrant Fund	258,402.50
From Tax on Sealskins	817,452.75
From Deposits by Individuals for Surveying Public Lands	94,289.76
From Revenues of the District of Columbia	2,367,869.01
From Miscellaneous Sources	1,458,672.04
Total Ordinary Receipts	371,403,277.66

ANALYSIS OF UNITED STATES EXPENDITURES FOR THE YEAR ENDING JUNE 30, 1887.

For Civil Expenses	$ 22,072,436.27
For Foreign Intercourse	7,104,490.47
For Indian Service	6,194,522.69
For Pensions	75,029,101.79
For the Military Establishment, including Rivers and Harbors and Arsenals	38,561,025.85
For the Naval Establishment, including Vessels. Machinery and Improvements at Navy Yards	15,141,126.80
For Miscellaneous Expenditures, including Public Buildings, Light-houses and collecting the Revenue	52,002,647.46
For Expenditures on Account of the District of Columbia	4,085,251.39
For Interest on the Public Debt	47,741,577.25
For the Sinking Fund	47,903,248.15
Total Ordinary Expenditures	315,835,428.12

RECEIPTS OF THE UNITED STATES, BY YEARS, FOR THIRTY YEARS—FROM CUSTOMS, INTERNAL REVENUE AND OTHER SOURCES.

YEARS.	CUSTOMS.	INTERNAL REVENUE.	ALL OTHER SOURCES.	TOTAL NET ORDINARY RECEIPTS, (EXCLUDING LOANS)
1859	$ 49,565,824		$ 3,211,283	$ 52,777,107
1860	53,187,512		2,867,088	56,054,600
1861	39,582,126		1,894,174	41,476,300
1862	49,056,398		2,862,864	51,919,262
1863	69,059,642	37,640,788	5,394,515	112,094,945
1864	102,316,153	109,741,134	31,355,684	243,412,971
1865	84,928,261	209,464,215	27,638,682	322,031,158
1866	179,046,652	309,226,813	31,776,099	520,049,564
1867	176,417,811	266,027,537	20,401,332	462,846,680
1868	164,464,600	191,087,589	20,882,265	376,434,454
1869	180,048,427	158,356,461	18,783,369	357,188,257
1870	194,538,374	184,899,756	16,521,703	395,959,833
1871	206,270,408	143,098,154	25,062,543	374,431,105
1872	216,370,287	130,642,178	17,681,765	364,694,230
1873	188,089,523	113,729,314	20,358,837	322,177,674
1874	163,103,834	102,409,785	34,427,472	299,941,091
1875	157,167,722	110,007,494	16,845,555	284,020,771
1876	148,071,985	116,700,732	25,293,568	290,066,285
1877	130,956,493	118,630,408	31,513,741	281,100,642
1878	130,170,680	110,581,625	16,712,471	257,464,776
1879	137,250,048	113,561,611	21,510,478	272,322,137
1880	186,522,065	124,009,374	22,995,063	333,526,502
1881	198,159,676	135,264,386	27,358,231	360,782,293
1882	220,410,730	146,497,595	36,616,924	403,525,249
1883	214,706,497	144,720,369	38,860,716	398,287,582
1884	195,067,490	121,586,073	31,866,288	348,519,851
1885	181,471,939	112,498,726	29,720,041	323,690,706
1886	192,905,023	116,805,936	26,728,767	336,439,726
1887	217,286,893	118,823,391	35,293,033	371,403,317
1888				*390,000,000

*Official estimates, based on actual receipts for 8 months of the fiscal year.

EXPENDITURES OF THE UNITED STATES FOR THIRTY YEARS.

YEARS.	CIVIL AND MISCELLANEOUS.	WAR.	NAVY.	INDIANS.	PENSIONS.	INTEREST.	TOTAL.
1859	$23,797,544	$ 23,154,720	$ 14,690,928	$3,490,535	$1,222,223	$ 2,637,650	$ 68,993,600
1860	27,977,978	16,472,203	11,514,650	2,991,122	1,100,802	3,144,121	63,200,876
1861	23,327,288	23,001,531	12,387,157	2,865,487	1,034,600	4,034,157	66,650,213
1862	21,385,863	389,173,562	42,640,353	2,327,948	852,170	13,190,345	469,570,241
1863	23,198,392	603,314,412	63,261,235	3,152,033	1,078,513	24,729,701	718,734,276
1864	27,572,217	690,391,049	85,704,964	2,629,976	4,985,474	53,685,422	864,969,102
1865	42,989,383	1,030,690,408	122,617,434	5,059,361	16,347,621	77,395,090	1,295,099,289
1866	40,613,114	283,154,676	43,295,662	3,295,729	15,605,550	133,067,625	519,022,356
1847	51,110,224	95,224,416	31,034,011	4,642,592	20,936,552	143,781,592	346,729,327
1868	53,009,868	123,246,619	25,775,503	4,100,682	23,782,387	140,424,046	370,839,135
1869	56,474,061	78,501,991	20,000,758	7,042,923	28,476,622	130,694,243	321,190,598
1870	53,237,462	57,655,675	21,780,230	3,407,938	28,340,202	129,235,498	293,657,005
1871	60,481,916	35,799,992	19,431,027	7,426,997	34,443,859	125,576,566	283,160,357
1872	60,984,757	35,372,157	21,249,810	7,061,729	28,533,403	117,357,840	270,559,696
1873	73,328,110	46,323,138	23,526,257	7,951,705	29,359,427	104,750,688	285,239,325
1874	85,141,594	42,313,927	30,932,587	6,692,462	29,038,415	107,119,815	301,238,800
1875	71,070,703	41,120,646	21,497,626	8,384,657	29,456,216	103,093,545	274,623,393
1876	73,599,661	38,070,889	18,963,310	5,966,558	28,257,396	100,243,271	265,101,085
1877	58,926,533	37,082,736	14,959,935	5,277,007	27,963,752	97,124,512	241,334,475
1878	53,177,701	32,154,148	17,365,301	4,629,286	27,137,019	102,500,975	236,964,327
1879	65,741,555	40,425,661	15,125,127	5,206,109	35,121,482	105,327,949	266,947,883
1880	54,713,530	38,116,916	13,536,985	5,945,457	56,777,174	95,757,575	264,847,637
1881	64,416,325	40,466,461	15,686,672	6,514,161	50,059,280	82,508,741	259,651,640
1882	57,219,751	43,570,494	15,032,046	9,736,747	61,345,194	71,077,207	257,981,439
1883	68,678,022	43,911,383	15,283,437	7,362,590	66,012,574	59,160,131	265,408,187
1884	70,920,434	39,429,603	17,292,601	6,475,999	55,429,228	54,573,378	244,126,243
1885	87,494,253	42,670,578	16,021,080	6,552,495	56,102,267	51,386,257	260,226,935
1886	74,166,930	34,324,153	13,907,888	6,099,158	63,404,864	50,580,146	242,483,139
1887	85,264,825	38,561,026	15,141,127	6,194,523	75,029,102	47,741,577	267,932,180
1883							*309,000,000

* Official estimate based upon actual receipts for 8 months of the fiscal year.

ANALYSIS OF INTEREST-BEARING PUBLIC DEBT, JAN. 1, 1887, AND JAN. 1, 1888.

DESCRIPTION.	OUTSTANDING JAN. 1, 1887.	OUTSTANDING JAN. 1, 1888.	DECREASE.
Bonds at 4½ per cent., payable 1891	$250,000,000	$230,544,600	$19,455,400
Bonds at 4 per cent., payable 1907	737,971,950	732,593,630	5,378,320
Bonds at 3 per cent., matured	63,899,000	*all paid.*	63,899,000
Navy Pension Fund	14,000,000	14,000,000	....
Bonds known as "Currency 6 per cents."	64,623,512	64,623,512	....
TOTAL	$1,130,494,462	$1,041,761,742	$88,732,720

DISPOSITION OF SURPLUS FOR YEAR ENDING JUNE 30, 1887.

The Excess of Receipts over ordinary Expenditures for the year was..$55,567,849.54
The above amount, together with a sum taken from previous cash balance in the treasury amounting to........ 24,455,720.46

        Making a total of.............................$80,023,570.00
Was applied to the redemption of the matured 3 per cent. bonds to the amount of.............................$79,864,100.00
And to the redemption of outstanding matured bonds of various old issues to the amount of ....$ 159,470.00

                                                                                               $80,023,570.00

THE SURPLUS.—NET CASH IN TREASURY BY MONTHS DURING CURRENT FISCAL YEAR.

July 1, 1887	$ 40,853,369
August 1, 1887	45,698,594
September 1, 1887	44,760,908
October 1, 1887	45,269,665
November 1, 1887	56,758,704
December 1, 1887	55,258,701
January 1, 1888	69,842,879
February 1, 1888	85,230,746
March 1, 1888	92,987,796
April 1, 1888	104,573,930
May 1, 1888	110,244,969

STATEMENT OF AMOUNT OF INTEREST-BEARING PUBLIC DEBT FOR THIRTY YEARS AND ANNUAL INTEREST CHARGE.*

YEAR.	TOTAL OUTSTANDING INTEREST-BEARING DEBT.	ANNUAL INTEREST CHARGE.
1859 (July 1.)	$ 58,290,738	$ 3,126,166
1860	64,640,838	3,443,687
1861	90,380,873	5,092,630
1862	365,304,826	22,048,509
1863	707,531,634	41,854,148
1864	1,359,930,763	78,853,487
1865	2,221,311,918	137,742,617
1865 (Aug. 31.)	2,381,530,294	150,977,697
1866	2,332,331,207	146,068,196
1867	2,248,067,387	138,892,450
1868	2,202,088,727	128,459,598
1869	2,162,060,522	125,523,998
1870	2,046,455,722	118,784,960
1871	1,934,696,750	111,949,330
1872	1,814,794,100	103,988,463
1873	1,710,483,950	98,049,804
1874	1,738,930,750	98,796,004
1875	1,722,676,300	96,855,690
1876	1,710,685,450	95,104,261
1877	1,711,888,500	93,160,643
1878	1,794,735,650	94,654,472
1879	1,797,643,700	83,773,778
1880	1,72 ,993,100	79,633,981
1881	1,639,567,750	75,018,695
1882	1,463,810,400	57,360,110
1883	1,338,229,150	51,436,709
1884	1,226,563,850	47,926,432
1885	1,196,150,950	47,014,133
1886	1,146,014,100	45,510,098
1887	1,021,692,350	41,780,529
1888*	1,041,764,052	

*Debt Statement April 2, 1888.

LEADING ARTICLES OF IMPORTS, 1887.

The following table shows the values of the leading and all other articles of imported merchandise entered for consumption in the United States, including both entries for immediate consumption and withdrawals from warehouse for consumption, during the year ending June 30, 1887:

FREE OF DUTY.

Order.	Articles.	Values.
		Dollars.
1	Coffee	56,360,701.42
2	Chemicals, drugs, dyes, and medicines	27,025,787.62
3	Hides and skins, other than fur-skins	24,225,776.21
4	Silk, unmanufactured, cocoons, eggs, etc.	19,640,397.00
5	Tea	16,373,422.66
6	India-rubber and gutta-percha, crude	13,762,627.00
7	Tin, bars, blocks, or pigs, grain or granulated	6,927,710.00
8	Fruits, including nuts	4,767,628.58
9	Paper stock, crude	4,538,719.21
10	Ores, (emery, gold and silver)	3,840,925.00
11	Wood, unmanufactured	3,550,191.83
12	Spices, unground	3,315,964.92
13	Animals	3,136,081.52
14	Household effects, etc., of immigrants	2,659,700.47
15	Furs and fur-skins, undressed	2,471,279.60
16	Hair	2,404,423.00
17	Eggs	1,960,405.39
18	Fertilizers	1,773,367.98
19	Oils, fixed or expressed and volatile or essential	1,736,239.58
20	Cocoa, or cacao, crude, leaves and shells of	1,670,008.00
21	Cork wood, or cork bark, unmanufactured	1,239,247.00
22	Fish	1,098,561.82
23	Books and other printed matter	968,466.21
24	Farinaceous substances, preparations of	721,984.16
25	Ivory, unmanufactured	631,031.00
26	Seeds	596,522.05
27	Cotton, unmanufactured	533,219.00
28	Platina or platinum	497,441.00
29	Art works, the production of American artists	495,936.50
30	Hide-cuttings, raw, and all glue stock	485,042.00
31	Plumbago	331,621.00
32	Diamonds, rough or uncut, dust and glaziers'	304,882.00
33	Tanning materials	292,090.00
34	Sausage skins	278,140.00
35	Bolting-cloths	271,693.00
36	Plants, trees, shrubs, and vines of all kinds, not elsewhere specified	254,472.45
37	Hoofs, horns, and parts of horns, unmanufactured, and horn strips and tips	235,249.50
38	Cabinets of coins, medals, and all other collections of antiquities	231,370.00
39	Feathers for beds and downs	204,961.55

LEADING ARTICLES OF IMPORTS—Continued.

FREE OF DUTY.

Order.	Articles.	Values.
		Dollars.
40	Articles, the growth, production, etc., of the United States, exported and brought back..................	8,485,813.94
41	Articles from the Hawaiian Islands, free under reciprocity treaty..	9,654,048.00
42	All other free articles................................	3,140,509.98
	Total free of duty	$233,093,659.15

DUTIABLE.

Order.	Articles.	Values.	Ordinary duties collected.	Average ad valorem rates of duty.
1	Sugar, confectionary, and molasses:	*Dollars.*	*Dollars.*	*Per cent*
	Molasses	5,336,729.63	1,496,863.32	28.05
	Sugar and confectionary....	68,905,549.57	56,519,823.02	82.03
	Total................	74,242,279.20	58,016,686.34	78.15
2	Wool, and manufactures of:			
	Wool, raw................	16,351,369.97	5,899,816.63	36.08
	Manufactures of..........	44,235,243.64	29,729,717.50	67.21
	Total................	60,586,613.61	35,629,534.13	58.81
3	Iron and steel, and manufactures of:			
	Iron ore	2,112,128.00	855,995.83	40.53
	Pig iron	6,510,126.08	2,811,026.05	43.18
	Manufactures of	41,996,731.52	17,046,212.01	40.59
	Total................	50,618,985.60	20,713,233.89	40.92
4	Flax, hemp, jute, etc., and manufactures of:			
	Unmanufactured—			
	Flax	1,908,845.00	154,508.63	8.09
	Hemp, jute, sisal grass, and other vegetable substances............	9,971,276.00	1,775,831.39	17.81
	Manufactures of	21,927,161.55	7,567,641.72	34.52
	Total	33,807,282.55	9,497,981.74	28,10

LEADING ARTICLES OF IMPORTS—Continued.
DUTIABLE.

Order.	Articles.	Values.	Ordinary duties collected.	Average ad valorem rates of duty.
		Dollars.	Dollars.	per cent
5	Silk, manufactures of	31,264,276.58	15,540,300.70	49.71
6	Cotton, manufactures of	29,150,058.83	11,710,719.88	40.17
7	Fruits, including nuts	15,088,073.82	4,210,098.64	27.90
8	Chemicals, drugs, dyes, and medicines	13,285,225.75	4,654,165.24	35.03
9	Jewelry and precious stones	10,981,191.66	1,162,300.19	10.58
10	Tobacco, and manufactures of	10,955,125.03	9,127,758.26	83.32
11	Leather, and manufactures of	10,933,569.77	3,286,862.17	30.06
12	Liquors: Malt, spirituous, and wines—			
	Malt liquors	1,267,309.25	614,186.73	48.47
	Spirits, distilled	1,909,899.96	2,939,923.04	154.01
	Wines	7,013,737.19	3,848,133.05	54.90
	Total	10,190,946.40	7,402,242.82	72.63
13	Wood, and manufactures of:			
	Unmanufactured	15,087.39	2,977.26	19.73
	Manufactures of	8,208,416.67	1,500,206.83	18.28
	Total	8,223,504.06	1,503,184.09	18.28
14	Glass and glassware	7,801,339.78	4,510,312.48	59.01
15	Fancy articles	7,185,999.95	2,949,360.14	41.04
16	Breadstuffs	6,386,560.72	1,075,811.24	16.84
17	Earthen, stone, and china-ware	5,708,093.40	3,251,881.22	56.97
18	Hats, bonnets, and hoods, and materials for	4,902,911.07	1,051,609.00	21.41
19	Animals	4,665,066.51	933,013.30	20.00
20	Furs, and manufactures of	4,545,265.24	926,217.73	20.38
21	Buttons and button materials	3,772,927.25	897,645.17	23.79
22	Hops	3,117,662.70	1,329,506.31	42.64
23	Metals, metal compositions, and manufactures of	2,988,882.51	962,785.71	32.21
24	Fish	2,817,351.73	611,937.69	21.72
25	Coal and coke	2,811,158.31	683,728.46	24.32
26	Books, maps, engravings, etchings, etc.	2,736,137.70	684,004.10	25.00
27	Vegetables	2,276,304.47	547,509.90	24.05
28	Paper, and manufactures of	1,985,264.86	424,618.27	21.39
29	Art works: Paintings and statuary	1,925,905.87	577,771.75	30.00
30	Clocks and watches, & parts of	1,892,564.05	489,325.83	25.90

LEADING ARTICLES OF IMPORTS—Continued.
DUTIABLE.

Order.	Articles.	Values.	Ordinary duties collected.	Average ad valorem rates of duty.
		Dollars.	*Dollars.*	*per cent*
31	Provisions, comprising meat and dairy products........	1,759,163.45	429,987.42	24.44
32	Musical instruments	1,613,883.78	403,470.95	25.00
33	Rice........................	1,518,766.10	971,454.89	64.01
34	Salt	1,455,385.18	676,865.50	49.92
35	Paints and colors	1,220,806.26	399,532.99	32.78
36	Bristles	1,156,435.00	174,423.71	15.03
37	Cement, Roman, Portland, and all other.............	1,102,532.41	220,506.48	20.00
38	Oils, animal, mineral and vegetable................	1,067,145.98	269,926.60	25.31
39	Corsets and corset cloth....	1,058,793.00	370,577.55	35.00
40	Marble and stone, and manufactures of	960,981.64	381,405.48	39.69
41	Matting and mats for floors.	885,968.75	177,193.75	20.00
42	Seeds	846,580.84	172,437.68	20.36
43	Hay	791,686.75	157,444.53	18.89
44	Brushes	557,347.54	167,204.26	30.00
45	Paper pulp, dried, for paper-makers' use	497,275.45	49,727.34	10.00
46	Glue	479,756.00	95,951.20	20.00
47	Gold and silver, manufactures of................	440,707.99	132,067.87	29.97
48	Soap	436,223.96	117,130.52	26.89
49	Gun powder and all explosive substances...............	423,955.00	368,137.10	86.83
50	Brass, and manufactures of.	405,755.81	170,937.70	42.15
51	Lead, and manufactures of.	346,623.35	236,617.78	68.26
52	Grease	324,486.66	52,349.97	16.13
	Copper:			
53	Unmanufactured	212,646.00	105,887.20	49.80
54	Manufactures of.........	111,099.60	23,069.88	44.14
	Total..	323,745.60	128,957.08	48.68
55	Sponges	302,509.57	60,501.91	20.00
56	Clays and earths............	286,768.24	89,884.18	31.34
57	Zinc, and manufactures of.	286,156.65	140,313.54	49.03
58	India-rubber and gutta-percha, manufactures of.	263,743.55	76,047.94	28.83
59	Carriages, and parts of.....	242,998.72	85,049.55	35.00
60	Corks, and cork-bark, manufactured.................	209,531.58	52,382.90	25.00
	Hair:			
	Unmanufactured........	103,852.28	24,839.23	23.92
	Manufactures of.......	96,906.09	30,418.58	31.39
	Total.....	200,758.37	55,257.81	27 52

LEADING ARTICLES OF IMPORTS—Concluded.

DUTIABLE.

Order.	Articles.	Values.	Ordinary duties collected.	Average ad valorem rates of duty.
		Dollars.	Dollars.	per cent.
61	Mineral substances, not elsewhere specified	191,295.84	24,025.83	12.25
62	Saddlery, coach, and harness hardware, etc.	184,258.83	64,490.58	35.00
63	Spices, ground	170,303.70	66,271.12	38.91
64	Chicory root, ground or unground, burnt or prepared	163,682.00	106,671.70	65.17
65	Ginger ale or ginger beer	153,376.54	30,675.30	20.00
66	Umbrellas, parasols, shades, and parts of	152,742.27	62,186.71	40.71
67	Cocoa, prepared, and cocoa butter	144,905.92	12,692.69	8.76
68	Inks of all kinds and ink powder	103,658.81	31,097.64	30.00
69	All other dutiable articles	1,258,096.98	388,455.87	30.88
	Total dutiable	450,325,321.55	212,032,423.90	47.10
	Total free of duty	233,093,659.15		
	Additional and discriminating duty		a 2,189,885.75	
	Total	683,418,980.70	214,222,309.65	

a Of this amount $1,996,528.49 was duty equal to unpaid internal revenue tax on domestic spirits and tobacco brought back.

TABLE SHOWING RELATIVE VALUES OF PRINCIPAL CLASSES OF FREE AND DUTIABLE IMPORTS, AND THE RELATION OF THE DUTY ON EACH CLASS TO ITS VALUE.

Classes.	Dollars.	Per cent. of total.
FREE OF DUTY.	*Value.*	*Value.*
(A) Articles of food, and animals	99,183,773	14.51
(B) Articles in a crude condition which enter into the various processes of domestic industry	106,389,032	15.57
(C) Articles wholly or partially manufactured, for use as materials in the manufactures and mechanic arts	12,149.883	1.78
(D) Articles manufactured, ready for consumption	11,565.665	1.69
(E) Articles of voluntary use, luxuries, etc.	3,805,306	.56
Total	233,093,659	34.11
DUTIABLE.		
(A) Articles of food, and animals	112,273,076	16.43
(B) Articles in a crude condition which enter into the various processes of domestic industry	59,542,660	8.71
(C) Articles wholly or partially manufactured, for use as materials in the manufactures and mechanic arts	67,505,441	9.88
(D) Articles manufactured, ready for consumption	124,473,106	18.21
(E) Articles of voluntary use, luxuries, etc.	86,531,039	12.66
Total	450,325,322	65.89
DUTIABLE.	*Duty.*	*Duty.*
(A) Articles of food, and animals	67,998,334	32.07
(B) Articles in a crude condition which enter into the various processes of domestic industry	19,567,903	9.23
(C) Articles wholly or partially manufactured, for use as materials in the manufactures and mechanic arts	20,393,493	9.62
(D) Articles manufactured, ready for consumption	61,899,366	29.19
(E) Articles of voluntary use, luxuries, etc.	42,174,328	19.89
Total	212,032,424	100.00

PERCENTAGES OF TOTAL DUTY PAID BY LEADING ARTICLES AND CLASSES OF IMPORTS.*

The following table shows the per cent. of the total duty collected in various years from 1867 to 1887, inclusive, on the leading articles of dutiable imports. The duty collected on the eleven articles and classes of articles named in the table has varied during the period named from 68 per cent. to 81 per cent. of the total duty collected annually on all articles.

Sugar is the leading article from which our customs revenue is collected, followed by manufactures of wool, manufactures of iron and steel, manufactures of silk, and manufactures of cotton, in the order named.

Per cent. of total duty collected on the leading articles and classes of articles of imported merchandise from 1867 to 1887, inclusive:

Articles and classes of articles.	1867.	1870.	1873.	1874.	1875.	1876.	1877.	1879.	1881.	1882.	1884.	1886.	1887.
	Pr. ct.	Pr. ct.	Pr. ct.	Pr. ct.	Pr. ct.	Pr. ct.	Pr. ct.	Pr. ct.	Pr. ct.	Pr. ct.	Pr. ct.	Pr. ct.	Pr. ct.
Sugar, confection'y, & molasses	19.35	21.23	17.33	21.72	24.04	28.86	28.88	30.20	24.76	22.77	25.71	29.29	27.36
Wool:													
Unmanufactured	1.16	1.16	4.24	2.78	2.35	1.92	2.07	1.47	2.51	1.46	2.37	1.78	2.78
Manufactures of	14.46	12.46	16.57	17.35	17.65	15.51	13.70	12.62	11.57	11.75	14.39	13.64	14.02
Iron and steel, and manuf'r's of	7.74	7.90	9.86	6.80	4.41	3.21	2.92	2.76	11.07	11.19	7.78	6.72	9.77
Flax, Hemp, Jute, etc.:													
Unmanufactured	.38	.37	.48	.41	.53	.73	.71	.86	.79	.77	.88	1.09	.91
Manufactures of	4.97	3.49	3.42	4.41	4.42	4.07	4.55	4.50	3.98	3.77	4.07	4.00	3.57
Silk, manufactures of	6.53	7.27	9.35	8.84	9.08	9.56	9.96	10.51	9.82	10.47	9.97	7.86	7.33
Cotton, manufactures of	5.68	4.80	6.25	5.63	5.85	5.50	5.10	4.93	5.58	5.66	6.03	6.14	5.52
Tobacco, and manufactures of	1.34	1.91	3.40	3.83	3.41	3.24	3.40	3.19	2.40	2.78	3.65	4.13	4.30
Liquors, spirituous and malt, and wines	4.28	4.35	5.07	5.33	4.86	4.47	4.58	4.10	3.52	3.32	3.29	4.02	3.49
Chemicals, drugs, dyes, and medicines	2.43	2.46	1.78	1.95	2.13	2.00	2.40	2.57	2.39	2.31	1.95	2.13	2.20
All other merchandise	31.68	32.60	22.25	20.95	21.27	20.93	21.70	22.29	21.61	23.75	19.91	19.20	18.75
Total	100.00	100.00	100.00	100.00	100.00	100.00	100.00	100.00	100.00	100.00	100.00	100.00	100.00

*Compiled by U. S. Bureau of Statistics.

ANALYSIS OF INTERNAL REVENUE RECEIPTS.

Objects of Taxation.	Receipts during fiscal year ended June 30—	
	1886.	1887.
SPIRITS.		
Spirits distilled from apples, peaches, and grapes	$ 1,400,394.48	$1,090,879.07
Spirits distilled from materials other than apples, peaches, and grapes	62,365,825.13	59,551,972.59
Rectifiers (special tax)	178,650.17	176,600.12
Retail liquor-dealers (special tax)	4,714,735.18	4,587,268.21
Wholesale liquor dealers (special tax)	418,406.24	416,304.66
Manufacturers of stills (special tax)	1,102.90	860.86
Stills and worms manufactured (special tax)	3,000.00	2,860.00
Stamps for distilled spirits intended for exports	10,151.90	3,076.20
Total	69,092,266.00	65,829,321.71
TOBACCO.		
Cigars and cheroots	10,532,804.05	11,364,916.83
Cigarettes	655,569.55	792,279.60
Snuff	493,233.80	524,942.26
Tobacco, chewing and smoking	14,834,095.42	15,995,019.46
Dealers in leaf-tobacco (special tax)	53,875.63	51,891.14
Dealers in manufactured tobacco (special tax)	1,208,529.17	1,245,412.65
Manufacturers of tobacco (special tax)	5,575.85	5,563.75
Manufacturers of cigars (special tax)	108,695.45	113,340.00
Peddlers of tobacco (special tax)	14,933.61	14,701.94
Total	27,907,362.53	30,108,067.13
FERMENTED LIQUORS.		
Ale, beer, lager-beer, porter, and other similar fermented liquors	19,157,612.87	21,387,411.79
Brewers (special tax)	186,928.89	187,352.24
Retail dealers in malt liquors (special tax)	169,502.56	177,148.13
Wholesale dealers in malt liquors (special tax)	162,686.97	170,275.33
Total	19,676,731.29	21,922,187.49
Oleomargarine		723,948.04
Miscellaneous, including Penalties	226,509.62	253,776.69
Total receipts	116,902,869.44	118,837,301.06

ESTIMATE OF EFFECT OF THE PROPOSED "MILLS BILL" ON REVENUES, BASED ON IMPORTATIONS OF 1887.*

FREE LIST.

	IMPORTATIONS OF 1887.	
	Values.	Duties.
Wood, salt, hemp, chemicals, metals, etc.	$61,672,120.42	$16,799,450.75
Wool	18,206,987.97	5,390,054.73
Total free list	79,879,108.39	22,189,595.48

SCHEDULES (DUTIABLE).

	IMPORTATIONS OF 1887.		ESTIMATED		AVERAGE AD VALOREM UNDER	
	Values.	Duties.	Duties under proposed bill.	Amount of duties remitted.	Present. Per cent.	Proposed. Per cent.
A. Chemicals	$5,050,825.28	$2,012,120.51	$1,133,846.78	$ 878,273.73	39.84	22.45
B. Earthenware & glassware	10,492,067.82	6,920,108.16	5,163,820.44	1,756,287.72	65.96	49.21
C. Metals	16,152,789.24	8,456,847.29	6,976,374.70	1,480,472.59	52.35	43.19
D. Wood and woodenware	889,558.56	307,805.13	260,217.95	47,587.18	34.60	29.25
E. Sugar	68,897,102.27	56,515,601.67	45,223,513.73	11,292,087.94	82.04	65.64
F. Tobacco	26,441.00	21,567.00	10,064.60	11,502.40	81.57	38.06
G. Provisions	3,235,987.68	1,711,805.92	1,380,320.92	331,485.00	52.89	42.65
I. Cotton and cotton goods	2,423,585.23	1,233,599.57	955,989.28	277,610.29	50.90	40.00
J. Hemp, jute, and flax goods	17,434,514.05	6,228,310.41	4,185,954.62	2,042,355.79	35.72	24.01
K. Wool and woollens	42,418,127.04	29,256,442.90	16,925,861.70	12,330,581.20	68.92	39.87
M. Books, papers, etc.	57,298.01	13,982.25	10,425.35	3,556.90	24.40	18.19
N. Sundries	11,221,253.04	4,984,936.33	3,905,795.33	1,079,141.00	44.42	34.79
Total dutiable	178,329,048.72	117,663,127.14	86,132,185.40	31,530,941.74	65.98	48.30
Total free list	79,879,108.39	22,189,505.48		22,189,505.48	27.78	
Total tariff reductions	258,208,157.11	139,852,632.62	86,132,185.40	53,720,447.22	54.16	33.36
Total int'l. rev. reduction				24,455,607.00		
Total proposed reduction				79,176,054.22		

*This table was prepared as a part of the report of Mr. Mills as chairman of the Ways and Means Committee, April 2, 1888, accompanying the tariff bill.

ESTIMATED REDUCTION OF INTERNAL TAXATION UNDER THE PROVISIONS OF "A BILL TO REPEAL CERTAIN TOBACCO AND OTHER TAXES, AND TO MODIFY INTERNAL-REVENUE LAWS."*

Total receipts from tobacco, fiscal year 1887		$30,108,067
Deduct cigars and cigarettes	$12,157,196	
Deduct special taxes manufacturers of cigars .... 18,570 × $3 =	55,710	
Deduct special taxes dealers in tobacco .... 514,000 × $1 =	514,000	
		12,726,906
Receipts from proposed repealed sources, fiscal year 1887		17,381,161
The increase in the receipts of that part of the tobacco tax which this bill proposes to repeal during the first seven months of the current fiscal year over the receipts for the corresponding period of the last fiscal year was $1,234,101, or 13 per cent. Assuming that this rate of increase will continue to the close of the fiscal year, the receipts from these objects of taxation would be increased		2,259,551
Special taxes retail liquor dealers, fiscal year 1887		4,587,268
Special taxes retail dealers in malt liquors, fiscal year 1887		177,148
Special taxes manufacturers of stills and stills manufactured, fiscal year 1887		3,721
Add for assessed penalties		41,758
Add for interest clause in section 10, say		5,000
Total estimated reduction		24,455,607

* This table was prepared by the Commissioner of Internal Revenue, March 12, 1888, at the request of Mr. Mills, and accompanies the report (April 2, 1888) of the majority of the Ways and Means Committee.

REVENUE REDUCTIONS SINCE THE WAR.*

Of internal taxes the following have been the reductions made since the conclusion of the war:

By the acts of July 13, 1866, and March 2, 1867	$103,81,199
By the acts of March 31, 1868, and February 3, 1868	54,802,578
By the act of July 14, 1870	55,315,321
By the act of December 21, 1871	14,436,862
By the act of June 6, 1872	15,807,618
By the acts of March 1, 1879, and May 28, 1880	6,368,935
By the act of March 3, 1883	40,677,682
Total	$290,790,195

From customs duties (according to estimates prepared when the several bills were passed) the following reductions of revenue have been made:

By the act of July 14, 1870: By additions to free list	$ 2,403,000
Ditto: Estimated reduction from dutiable list	23,651,748
Total	26,054,748
By the act of May 1, 1872, tea and coffee were placed upon the free list, making a reduction of	$ 15,893,847
By the act of June 6, 1872, tariff duties were further reduced as follows: By additions to free list	$ 3,345,724
Ditto: Estimated reduction from the dutiable list	11,933,191
Total	$ 15,278,915
By the act of March 3, 1883, were made the following reductions: By additions to free list	$ 1,365,999
Ditto: Estimated reduction from dutiable list	19,489,800
Total	$ 20,855,799

GENERAL FEATURES OF OUR EXPORT TRADE FOR THE YEAR ENDING JULY 1, 1887.

Articles.	Values.	Per cent.
Products of agriculture	$523,073,798	74.41
Products of manufacture	136,735,105	19.45
Products of mining (including mineral oils)	11,758,662	1.67
Products of the forest	21,126,273	3.01
Products of the fisheries	5,155,775	.73
Other products	5,173,310	.73
Total	703,022,923	100.00

* This table is taken from Mr. McKinley's minority report of the Ways and Means Committee on the so-called Mills' bills.

THE CARRYING TRADE IN UNITED STATES VESSELS AND ITS DECLINE.

The value of merchandise transported in the carrying trade of the United States during the year ending June 30, 1887, is shown as follows:

Carried in	Imports.	Exports.				a In transit and trans-shipment trade.	Total foreign commerce.	Per cent.
		Domestic.	Foreign.	Total.				
	Dollars.	Dollars.	Dollars.	Dollars.		Dollars.	Dollars.	
Cars and other land vehicles	27,562,059	18,784,852	2,604,814	21,389,666		18,754,082	67,705,807	4.53
American vessels:								
Steam	60,685,426	33,706,531	1,015,158	34,721,689		17,857,694	113,264,809	7.58
Sail	60,680,067	37,461,311	808,253	38,269,564		351,426	99,301,057	6.65
Total	121,365,493	71,167,912	1,823,411	72,991,253		18,209,120	212,565,666	14.23
Foreign vessels:								
Steam	476,170,712	493,884,766	7,597,930	501,482,696		47,054,696	1,024,708,094	68.59
Sail	67,221,504	119,185,463	1,134,133	120,319,596		1,514,354	189,055,454	12.65
Total	513,392,216	613,070,229	8,732,063	621,802,292		48,569,040	1,213,763,548	81.24
Grand total	692,319,768	703,022,923	13,160,288	716,183,211		85,532,242	1,494,035,221	100.00

a Received and shipped.

www.ingramcontent.com/pod-product-compliance
Lightning Source LLC
Chambersburg PA
CBHW020807230426
43666CB00007B/896